COLLECTING

CIGARETTE & TRADE CARDS

Gordon Howsden

New Cavendish Books

London

First edition published in Great Britain by
New Cavendish Books Ltd

American edition published by
Pincushion Press

Designed by Jacky Wedgwood

Edited by Narisa Chakra

Photography by Mark Williams
Copyright © on all photographs New Cavendish Books

Typesetting by Bartlett Rice Associates, London

Printed and bound in Hong Kong under the supervision of Mandarin Offset, London

New Cavendish Books Ltd.
3 Denbigh Road
London W11 2SJ

ISBN 1 872727 87 5 (UK edition)

Pincushion Press
6001 Johns Road
Tampa, FL 33634

ISBN 1 883685 05 2 (USA edition)

Acknowledgements

I would like to thank the many people and organisations who have contributed to the preparation of this book. In particular, the invaluable assistance given by the Cartophilic Society of Great Britain, whose reference books and magazines have been a major source of information. Also to Imperial Tobacco Limited for providing details of the history of the company and the tobacco industry.

On a personal level, thanks are due to Edward Wharton-Tigar, MBE, not only for writing the Foreword and allowing his Marquis of Lorne card to be illustrated, but also for much help and guidance. John Walton of the Cartophilic Society has been most generous with his time, as has Alan Harris, Hon Editor of *Cartophilic Notes & News*. Thanks also to John Dunn of ITL and Gerald Fletcher of *Art & Design*.

For non-technical assistance, I would like to thank Bill Price and Gillian Howsden for their unfailing support and encouragement. My grateful thanks are also given to the publisher, designer and photographer for their enthusiasm and hard work.

Finally, acknowledgement is made to Imperial Tobacco Limited and to all the other tobacco and trade companies whose cards and related material are illustrated in this book.

Author's note

Throughout the text the titles of card series are denoted in capital letters. Where series were issued without a title printed on the cards themselves, then an 'adopted' title has been used. The adopted titles conform to the World and British Trade Indexes and are denoted by the use of an asterisk.

The word 'series' sometimes forms part of the title and in these instances is denoted in capital letters. Where an issuer produced two or more series with the same title, a description in parentheses follows to assist with identification, eg RADIO CELEBRITIES (1st Series), or CINEMA STARS (Set 4).

The captions incorporate an approximate year of issue which is intended as a guide to when the cards were first issued. Illustrations generally depict the cards at about 95% of actual size. Some larger cards, however, have had to be further reduced in size.

COLLECTING
CIGARETTE &
TRADE CARDS

CONTENTS

FOREWORD

One of the best introductions to card collecting was written by my old friend Jefferson R Burdick of the USA in his book *The Standard Guide on all Collected Cards*, published in 1960. I quote a paraphrasing below:

"A Card Collection is a magic carpet that takes you away from work-a-day cares to havens of relaxing quietude where you can relive the pleasures and adventures of a past day – brought to life in vivid picture and prose. Here is a phase of our heritage without which history has no full meaning, and only history can help man to understand the past and present for the future. This is history from an original source.

Cards depict the devastation of nature's fury, the crashing armies of conquering nations, and the increasingly mad whirl of modern existence. They also show the serenity of a quiet country life, the gracious humility of those called great, the joyous romp of children on Christmas morning, and a thousand other homely things we love to remember. Every set of cards is a glorious picture window of the past. Pen, brush and camera have joined forces with the graphic arts to bring to life these groups of pictorial gems. Their important role in our past is now receiving a just recognition. History cannot ignore them and be complete."

Gordon Howsden has done an excellent job in presenting an outline of 'cartophily' and I commend it to those interested in our popular hobby.

E C Wharton-Tigar MBE
President of the Cartophilic Society of
Great Britain

INTRODUCTION

The practice of giving away picture cards as a sales promotion technique dates back well into the 19th century. The concept was certainly established on the Continent and in the USA many years before the first known cigarette card was issued. The picture card itself was a development of tradesmen's cards which date from the 17th century. The commercial application of the chromolithography method of printing during the middle of the 19th century boosted the growth of trade cards, so that by the 1870s a number of European firms, led by Au Bon Marché and Liebig, were issuing brightly coloured cards to purchasers of their products.

When cards were adopted by the tobacco companies they were first used for the practical purpose of protecting cigarettes from damage. The idea of using these cards, or 'stiffeners' as they were called in the trade, to carry advertisements soon caught hold and before long the concept had been developed into the distribution of a series of cards which would encourage the smoker to continue using that particular brand. The United States of America, less inhibited by tradition and with a culture based on enterprise and competition, was the birthplace of the cigarette card.

At a time when the average family could not afford books, and with the technique of reproducing photographs in newspapers still some years away, these cards could inform and amuse, and bring a little bit of colour into what were all too often very drab lives. And, of course, they were free – or as free as anything ever is that is 'given away' to promote the sale of a product. The British were a little slow to catch on to the possibilities of the cigarette card but once introduced it grew to become one of

the marketing success stories of the 20th century. Indeed, a whole industry developed around it and for four decades smokers could not conceive of opening a packet of cigarettes and not finding a card inside. Maybe they looked at it and tossed it away, perhaps it was given to one of the band of small boys who used cards for a variety of ingenious playground games, but often it was kept, treasured and mounted in one of the special albums sold by the tobacco manufacturers.

The boys, and some girls too, are not to be despised as, although they ruined many a fine card, the memory of those halcyon days of collecting remained in the subconscious and provided the seed corn for the next generation of serious collectors. The cigarette card became such a part of general life that even cards given away with tea, chocolates, groceries or periodicals were referred to by the issuers as 'cigarette cards'. But the cigarette card, of course, was just a form of trade card and trade cards are still as valuable for promotion purposes today, as they were 120 years ago.

The void left by the cessation of cigarette cards in 1940 was at first filled by cards issued with tea, candy sticks, cereals and chewing gum. But as the post-war years of austerity turned, for many at least, to the years of plenty, so the enterprising leaders of commerce realised there was a market for cards to be sold to collectors. As was the case in the 1880s, it was the Americans who were the first to exploit this potential and the commercial card market across the Atlantic is today turning over many millions of dollars annually.

This book is, however, mainly concerned with picture cards issued free with commodities.

Raleigh, the man who popularised smoking in England.
Pattreiouex **Builders of the British Empire**, c1929 (J, set of 50)

Liebig (F340), **Christopher Columbus**, 1892 (F, set of 6 extra large)

Naturally, a large part is devoted to the cigarette card as this developed the concept to an unprecedented level. But the importance of the trade card is recognised and there is also a brief excursion to look at silk pictures and other novelties issued by some of the tobacco manufacturers.

Any hobby is unlikely to progress very far without some organisation and a forum through which information can be shared and common problems discussed. For many years trade and cigarette cards were collected by enthusiasts who had no way of contacting each other, nor any formal means of exchanging or acquiring cards. The first collector to accept the challenge to do something about it was Colonel Charles Bagnall who in 1927 established The London Cigarette Card Company Ltd, which is still very active today. He issued catalogues listing sets of cards and prices which were accepted as a standard and he also introduced a magazine, *Cigarette Card News*, through which readers could share their views and pass on accumulated knowledge.

Cigarette card clubs started to spring up and in 1938 the Cartophilic Society of Great Britain was born. The declared aim of the Society today is '… to propagate, enhance and preserve the hobby of cigarette and trade card collecting'. Perhaps the greatest service rendered to the collector by the Society has been the many volumes of reference books produced by a very dedicated body of enthusiasts, none of whom has been more active than Mr E C Wharton-Tigar. But the Society is very much more than a collection of reference books, however valuable, as members and guests are always sure of a warm welcome at the meetings held by its 19 branches at various locations around the country.

For some reason items that cost nothing tend to be overlooked or even denigrated by our society. Despite the obvious attractiveness of cigarette and trade cards, there existed for over half a century a strong body of opinion that it was sheer stupidity to spend money on something that had been given away free. The very term 'cartophily', meaning love of cards, was coined by Colonel Bagnall to try and counter this view and to give card collectors a more respectable image. It is sad that this should have been necessary as the hobby was (and to some extent still is) one of the very few where the poor and anonymous participate on the same footing as the rich and famous.

Strong demand over the last twenty years, with no corresponding increase in supply, has seen prices of cards escalate rapidly. This is particularly noticeable among 19th century cards and items issued by the smaller tobacco companies. Of course, demand is not always rational and the scarcest items are not necessarily the most expensive. In the UK the most sought after set of cards is that known as CLOWNS AND CIRCUS ARTISTES* produced by the firm of Taddy & Co. It is doubtful if the cards were ever inserted in cigarette packets and the quality of printing is inferior to that of many of the other series bearing the Taddy name. But it is believed the set may have been the last planned for distribution by the firm before it closed down dramatically over a point of principle. The charisma that attaches to the few sets that are known to exist is such that they are guaranteed a high price whenever they appear at auction.

The most valuable card in the world to date is the 'Honus Wagner' baseball card, being one of a set of 524 issued by the American Tobacco Company in the USA between 1909 and 1911. The story goes that Wagner objected to his picture being used in connection with the sale of cigarettes and the card was withdrawn. Although there are scarcer cards, it is a Wagner card that every collector wants and in 1991 an example sold at auction for $451,000.

Fortunately, there are many hundreds of sets of cigarette cards that are available to the collector at very reasonable prices, bearing in mind their age and attractiveness. Trade cards, many of which were issued in quite limited numbers, can also be purchased economically, with many sets from the 1950s and 1960s available for a pound or two.

For new collectors there is an enormous wealth of material available which will give years of enjoyment. It is difficult, perhaps impossible, to explain in words the fascination of cigarette and trade cards and the satisfaction that can be obtained from collecting them. Hopefully, this book will give a taste of what is available and the stimulation to get out and start collecting. For those who are already hooked on this most excellent hobby the aim of this book is to help make collecting even more pleasurable by filling in some background information and generating new ideas.

Lea **More Lea's Smokers**, 1906 (H, per card) by artist Will Owen

PRICE GUIDE

The captions for each card, or set of cards, illustrated in this book includes a letter from A to K. A range of values has been attributed to each letter which at the date of publication gives the approximate price level of the item illustrated. The price guide relates to items in 'Very Good' condition as defined by the Cartophilic Society and includes an allowance for Value Added Tax at $17\frac{1}{2}$%. Demand for collectable items can change rapidly so collectors are advised to acquire one or more of the current price lists published by the major dealing houses.

A	up to £2	G	£30 to £50
B	£2 to £5	H	£50 to £75
C	£5 to £10	I	£75 to £100
D	£10 to £15	J	£100 to £150
E	£15 to £20	K	over £150
F	£20 to £30		

CHAPTER 1

TOBACCO AND THE CIGARETTE CARD

Player **Products of the World**, 1909 (C, set of 25)

The American Indians, possibly the first to use tobacco. Hudden **Types of Smokers**, c1903 (G, per card)

If it had not been for the tobacco companies, the collection of picture cards distributed free with commodities might well have remained an undeveloped, fringe pastime. The rapid growth and success of the manufacturers of tobacco products was in no small part due to the phenomenal popularity of the cigarette. And those who produced and sold their cigarettes most successfully were those who established branded products, who engendered customer loyalty and whose marketing strategies included the issue of cigarette cards.

Whether we like it or not, tobacco is a commodity of great importance to both the developed and the undeveloped countries of the world. Hundreds of thousands of people, either directly or indirectly, are employed to produce and process it, billions of pounds are spent in buying the end product and an enormous proportion of those billions find their way into National Exchequers to help fund Government spending.

TOBACCO

How this all came about and the part played by the cigarette card are stories that are both fascinating and instructive to the collector. Tobacco has certainly had a chequered history and has rarely had what might be termed 'official approval'. Many have been the attempts to curb or stamp out the use of tobacco products and sometimes the penalties have been violent in the extreme. But through it all the habit has persisted and the companies that process and market the end product have learnt through necessity the important art of survival.

The usual source of tobacco is *Nicotiana Tabacum*, a native plant of South America, which belongs to the *Solanaceae* family. This genus typically has tubular flowers with reflexed petals and incorporates the potato and tomato families and also several of the nightshades. Most experts believe that tobacco was initially used for religious purposes by the American Indians and that smoking as a ceremonial custom developed into use simply for relaxation and pleasure. The early explorers from Columbus onwards witnessed the use of tobacco, and the habit of smoking, snuffing and chewing was brought to Europe. Jean Nicot, the French Ambassador to Portugal in the 1560s, was an early enthusiast of the properties of tobacco and grew the plant in the gardens of the French Embassy.

Walter Raleigh is usually credited with introducing smoking to England in the early years of Queen Elizabeth's reign. It is certainly an attractive story although there is no concrete evidence to support the theory. Wills, in their series of HISTORIC EVENTS, state that Raleigh was the first person of note to smoke and picture him relaxing with his pipe. Certainly, by the end of the 16th century the custom of smoking had become widespread throughout the country. There were, however, those who abhorred the use of tobacco and in James I, who acceded to the English throne in 1603, they found a royal champion. He banned the growing of tobacco and in his publication *A Counterblaste to Tobacco* James referred to smoking as 'a custom loathsome to the eye, hateful to the nose, harmful to the brain, dangerous to the lungs' and generally did his best to stamp out the habit.

In other countries officialdom reacted even more strongly. Pope Urban VIII threatened

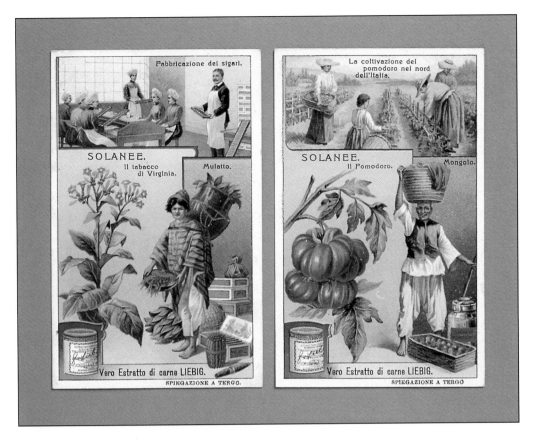

The tobacco plant has many relations including the tomato.
Liebig (F 973) **Solanaceae Family**, 1909 (C, set of six extra large)

Famous people connected with smoking

Left to right:
Wills **Historic Events**, 1912 (G, set of 50)
Player **Kings & Queens of England**, 1935 (G, set of 50)
Carrreras **Celebrities of British History**, 1935 (G, set of 50)

Smugglers resisting arrest. Ogden's **Smugglers and Smuggling**, 1932 (H, set of 50)

excommunication, the Swiss added prohibition of smoking to the Ten Commandments, in Russia the Tsar decreed that snuff takers should have their noses cut off and for offending Turks, Persians or Indians it was nothing less than the death penalty. But the habit persisted and in 1614 the English Star Chamber imposed a tax on tobacco, thus establishing the curious love-hate relationship for the product that has existed ever since.

The popularity of smoking, coupled with the ever increasing duties levied upon its importation, led inevitably to smuggling. When a Parliamentary Committee was set up by William Pitt in 1783, it was estimated that half the total amount of tobacco consumed had been illegally imported. Not only were the smugglers having a field day, so were the manufacturers, as the leaves of trees, herbs and other plants were added to the tobacco to defraud customer and Revenue alike. Pitt adopted a bonded warehouse system and placed all stocks of tobacco and its manufacture and processing under the control of Excise Officers. This was, in fact, an almost identical proposal to that suggested by Walpole some 50 years earlier, but never enacted due to vigorous opposition from the tobacco lobby.

To backtrack a little, we should note that by the end of the 17th century the firm of E & W Anstie of Devizes had been established as sellers of tobacco and snuff. In 1741 the firm of Stephen Mitchell & Son extended their existing grocery business by installing a snuff mill and a machine for cutting tobacco. During the next 50 years a number of firms were founded, such as Taddy & Co, R & J Hill and W D & H O Wills, and we shall meet them later in connection with the issue of cards.

CIGARETTES

The smoking of cigarettes is thought to have been introduced to the UK by soldiers returning from the Crimean War who had seen their Russian counterparts smoking tobacco rolled in tubes of thin paper. The pioneer credited with being the first to manufacture cigarettes in this country is Robert P Gloag, who had been in the Crimea as Paymaster to the Turkish Army. Such cigarettes were, of course, made by hand but a

A scene from the Crimean War. Ogden's **Victoria Cross Heroes**, c1901 (C, per card)

proficient person could produce around 250 cigarettes per hour. The concept of cigarette smoking had also made its way to North America but, as was the case with Britain, it was some years before it achieved any popularity. The American Civil War helped spread knowledge of the cigarette and by 1875 US Revenue statistics indicated production approaching 50 million. By 1877 the market had tripled, with Sweet Caporal from the firm of Kinney Bros, an early market leader. Other popular cigarettes of the time were manufactured by Allen & Ginter, Goodwin and Kimball.

At about this time James B Duke joined the family tobacco firm of W. Duke, Sons & Co and made a decision that the business should enter the growing cigarette market. He was fortunate to negotiate exclusive US rights to a new machine capable of manufacturing 200 cigarettes per minute and with this significant cost advantage set out to conquer the market.

Cigarette making machines in action. Wills **Irish Industries**, 1937 (G, set of 50)

By 1888 Duke claimed to be the nation's leading manufacturer with sales of 744 million cigarettes and by the mid-1890s every single manufacturer of note had joined or been absorbed by Duke's master company, the American Tobacco Company (ATC). Duke next turned his attention to the international market where his major competitors were the British manufacturers. So he decided to tackle the problem at source.

American cigarettes had been selling in Britain for some years through local agents and distributors but had little more than a toe-hold on the market. The firm of Wills had established itself as the dominant entity largely through their decision to mechanise cigarette production in 1883 but, unlike the situation in America, there had been no significant rationalisation among the various competing firms which numbered about 500. Duke made his move in the late summer of 1901. He sailed from New York to Liverpool, called on the local firm of Ogden's Limited and bought them out. Other manufacturers were approached, including John Player & Sons, where his greeting to J D and W G Player was, 'Hello boys, I'm Duke from New York come to take over your business'. In every case Duke was turned down flat and whilst he paused to consider his next step the British manufacturers acted.

THE TOBACCO WAR

Obviously, they must have had some inkling of a potential attack from across the Atlantic but even so the rapidity of their response was remarkable. Sir William Wills, Charles Lambert, Walter Butler and the Player brothers organised a meeting of the leading tobacco firms, which was held in Birmingham between 19 and 23 September. It cannot have been easy for these largely family controlled businesses to come to an agreement but finally a decision was reached and an application made to register the name 'The Imperial Tobacco Company (of Great Britain and Ireland) Limited'. The 13 founder members and the amounts paid by the ITC to purchase their businesses were as follows:

W D & H O Wills	£6,992,221
Hignett Bros	£477,038
Lambert & Butler	£754,306
William Clarke	£403,582
Adkin & Sons	£146,497
Richmond Cavendish	£313,805
Hignett's Tobacco	£54,183
Stephen Mitchell	£701,000
Franklyn, Davey	£473,555
F & J Smith	£525,803
Edwards, Ringer & Bigg	£372,603
D & J MacDonald	£134,973
John Player & Sons	£601,456

The size of the Wills business must have worried some of the smaller companies but the alternative to combining was even less pleasant. Each company had been assured that they could trade under their own name and retain responsibility for manufacturing and marketing.

Formal incorporation took place on 10 December 1901 with Sir William Wills elected chairman of a board of 25 directors that included no less than eight other members of the Wills family. The 'war' now began in earnest with each side trying to win the allegiance of both retailer and smoker. The ITC struck an early blow by acquiring the Salmon & Gluckstein retail business and then offered loyalty bonuses to other wholesalers and retailers. The initial tactics of Ogden's and the ATC had been to cut prices and issue coupons offering free gifts. This was in addition to Ogden's well advertised scheme for buying back complete albums of cards and donating them to hospitals. They also established a loyalty scheme of their own by offering stockists a share in the whole of Ogden's net profit for four years, plus a sum of £200,000 each year over the same period.

The ITC responded by opening up a new line of attack by sending a delegation to the USA to look for businesses to buy and thus confront the ATC in its home market. On 1 May 1902 four other British tobacco manufacturers joined the ITC including Churchman and Faulkner. It became clear to Duke that for once he had bitten off more than he could chew and he sued for peace. In September 1902 an agreement was negotiated whereby Ogden's was sold to the ITC and both the ITC and the ATC were restricted to their respective home markets. A new company, British-American Tobacco Company Limited (BAT), was established in London to acquire the trademarks, overseas subsidiaries and export businesses of both groups.

Subsequently, the US Courts decided in 1911 that the ATC was a trust acting against the public interest and ordered that it be broken up into four large independent firms. The ITC remained the dominant force in the British market throughout the cigarette card issuing period and in the 1930s were again at the forefront of a further battle to keep American influence out of their local market. On that occasion they acquired sufficient shares in

James B Duke, who founded the American Tobacco Company

Salmon & Gluckstein advertisement back, 1901

The Boer War, 1899-1902, enhanced the interest in cigarette cards.
Morris **Boer War 1900**, 1900 (G, per card)

Gallaher to prevent them from being taken over.

CIGARETTE CARDS

At the time of the Tobacco War cigarette cards had already been in existence for over 20 years. The companies that first put brand names on their cigarettes originally sold them loose or in flimsy paper packets. To stop the cigarettes from getting crushed a small piece of blank card was inserted in the packet and before long someone had the idea to use the card to advertise the company's products. This card was known as a stiffener and is still so referred to by the tobacco industry even today.

Who issued the first picture card will never be known for sure but for many years the earliest card to be dated accurately was an item depicting the Marquis of Lorne. This card was discovered by the great American collector, J R

The earliest cigarette card that can be accurately dated.
Marquis of Lorne Cigarettes, **Portrait of Marquis of Lorne***, 1879
(size 77 x 40mm)

Burdick, together with an advertisement for Marquis of Lorne cigarettes dated 1879.

The Marquis in question was the eldest son of the 8th Duke of Argyll and also the son-in-law of Queen Victoria, having in 1871 married her fourth daughter, Princess Louise. At the date of issue of the card he was Governor General of Canada but how or why his name came to be used on a packet of cigarettes is not known. In 1976, an even earlier American cigar card issued by R C Brown, was discovered by Mr Edward Wharton-Tigar, the picture of which depicted a gentleman holding a card dated 1877. The caption on the card was 'Happy New Year' thus dating it as issued in 1876.

The earliest cards issued in Britain were almost certainly packed with American cigarettes imported into the country. In her book *Collecting Cigarette Cards* Dorothy Bagnall illustrated a calendar card for 1884 issued by Allen & Ginter but showing on the reverse the British parcel post charges. This was very likely issued in 1883 and is the earliest card that can be accurately dated. The card was auctioned in 1981 and realised the handsome price of £510.

The largest British firm, W D & H O Wills, had started making cigarettes in 1871 with their Bristol brand and by 1878 the famous Three Castles and Gold Flake brands had been established. All were made by hand, as it was not until 1883 that the Bonsack cigarette making machine was introduced. The records of the Bristol printing firm of Mardon, Son & Hall, who were to join the Imperial group in 1902, indicated that a printed stiffener was produced for Wills in about 1887. Two or three years later another advertisement card was distributed showing a serving maid of the period on the front and listing 15 Wills' brands on the back.

It is possible that cards had been inserted in packets issued abroad before these dates but so far no definite proof is available. Equally, evidence may one day come to light that another British manufacturer had beaten Wills to it in issuing what we now call a cigarette card.

Both in the USA and Britain, the early advertisement type of card soon gave way to cards which formed part of a definite series. Smokers were almost exclusively male so most

Right:
Wills
Advertisement Cards*,
c1893 (K, per card)

Left:
Player
**Advertisement
Cards***, c1894
(K, per card)

virtually every manufacturer had a 'coupon' brand and cards took a back seat as smokers avidly saved to obtain gifts ranging from a hair brush to a three-piece suite. By 1933 profit margins had become so thin that certain manufacturers got together and agreed to outlaw gift schemes. And so in 1934 the 'coupon war' ended and cards were back in favour once more.

In terms of the number of collectors and quantities issued the following six years saw the cigarette card reach the peak of its popularity. But the end when it came was sudden. The Government quickly stepped in after war had been declared to stop what it considered a waste of valuable raw materials. This time there was to be no long term resumption on any meaningful scale after peace had been declared. Fortunately, Imperial Tobacco did decide in 1975 to pack cards with certain cigar brands and collectors applauded this enterprise. The cards currently being distributed with Castella cigars are of a quality comparable with the best that were produced in the 1920s and '30s. Although it currently seems unlikely that cards will ever again be issued with cigarettes, the possible restrictions threatened on advertising may yet see cards resume their former glory.

Gift schemes and coupons proliferated between 1928 and 1933

Carreras **Black Cat Gift Coupon**, c1930 (A, per coupon)

Modern cigar cards are of excellent quality

Wills Castella **Donington Collection**, 1993 (F, set of 30 large)

of the early series of cards featured actresses, music hall stars or, indeed, anyone with a pretty face. These pioneer items caused many problems for researchers as otherwise identical cards were often issued by several different firms, series were frequently reprinted with slight variations and individual cards were not always numbered.

Cigarette smoking and the use of cards expanded rapidly during the Edwardian period, being boosted especially by the Boer War and the Tobacco War. Even the advent of the 1914/18 conflict did not affect card issues other than to popularise military subjects and reflect patriotic sentiment. The shortage of paper and board led to cards being discontinued in 1917 and apart from one or two isolated series there was no general resumption until 1922.

Another hiccup occurred in the late 1920s when brands packing gift coupons began to take an ever increasing share of the market. By 1930

Churchman **Beauties 'CERF'***, c1904 (G, per card)

CHAPTER 2

A COLLECTOR'S GUIDE

One of the beauties of collecting cigarette and trade cards is that you can do it any way you please. It can be an adjunct to another hobby or activity or it can be an end in itself. The promotional aspect that led to cards being issued in the first place was, of course, that they could be collected in series or sets. This, indeed, is still the way the majority of enthusiasts go about collecting. Another popular way of collecting is to try and obtain a specimen, or 'type' as it is generally referred to, of each series of cards issued. This latter method is becoming the only sensible way a newcomer to the hobby can realistically hope to obtain a good general collection, especially of cards issued prior to 1905.

The increase in prices seen in the last 20 years has also resulted in a proliferation of reproductions. These are cards which are identical in every respect to the originals except that they state on the reverse that they are reprints. Another reason for their appearance is the growth in the market for framed cards, which apart from looking good in the living room, are widely used by pubs, clubs, hotels and restaurants. Reproductions are usually only purchased by serious collectors when the price of the originals is beyond their pocket.

Fortunately, the card world has not suffered too badly at the hands of the forger. They are about, however, and have been for the last 50 years. Caution should always be exercised especially if offered scarce cards at 'cheap' prices. If in doubt, members of the Cartophilic Society can send their cards to an expert panel who are able to adjudicate on whether or not a card is genuine. On the whole cigarette cards are not that expensive bearing in mind that they

have not been produced in the UK since 1940 and the huge wastage, particularly through juvenile games familiar to all 60 year olds. One of the reasons is that as the hobby became more organised in the early 1930s, some of the dealers were able to acquire large stocks of remainders from manufacturers and printers.

JARGON

The hobby is also relatively free of jargon or complicated terminology. Such as there is can usually be learned with a little experience. Collectors may initially be confused to read in the catalogues of series described as 'Actresses BLARM', 'Beauties CERF' or 'Boer War Generals CLAM'. The explanation is that when card issues started to become more widespread at the end of the 19th century, the cigarette manufacturers were reluctant to commit themselves to long print runs. The printing firms quickly realised that unit costs could be reduced if several manufacturers utilised the same series. The cards usually featured a pretty girl or a soldier on the front with the name of the manufacturer on the reverse. Invariably, the series were neither titled nor numbered.

When serious research started a code system was devised to distinguish these 'alike' series. The code works using the initial letters of some of the issuers so 'BLARM' stands for Baker, Lambert & Butler, Anonymous, Redford and Murray. The series of Actresses 'BLARM' used in this example was actually issued by nine firms. Frequently the front design was the same but the back would be printed to each issuer's individual order. Similarly, 'CERF' is taken from the initial letters of Churchman, Edwards, Ringer & Bigg and Franklyn, Davey & Co.

A Nostalgia reprint of Taddy's **Prominent Footballers**

The code letters in the adopted title help distinguish between untitled series issued by several manufacturers. Baker **Actresses BLARM***, c1900 (F, per card)

An 'Actress' card with the artiste named.
Pritchard & Burton **Actors and Actresses 'FROGA'*** (blue back), c1899
(D, per card)

page 19
Player produced many fine military and naval series
Left to right
Top row:
Military Series,1900
(D, per card)
Middle row, first and second cards:
Military Series,1900
(D, per card)
Middle row, third and fourth cards:
Old England's Defenders, c1898 (D, per card)
Bottom row:
Old England's Defenders, c1898 (D, per card)

Another convention is that sets given the adopted title of 'Actresses' generally have the name of the artiste printed on the card whereas the title 'Beauties' is usually given to sets where the ladies pictured are anonymous. Fortunately, untitled series were largely discontinued by 1905 but alike series continued to be produced by the constituent members of the larger groups.

CONDITION

An area where terminology is even more important is in the description of the quality or condition of cards. One famous collector before the 1939/45 war wrote an article in which he stated that there were three major points to consider when collecting cards. He then listed them as follows:

1 Condition. 2 Condition. 3 Condition.

Few collectors would disagree that more arguments and disputes are generated on this subject than on any other aspect of collecting cards. In a way it is only to be expected when, in the terminology of the hobby, a card described as 'good' does, in fact, have faults. Indeed, a number of collectors would probably never purchase a card so described unless it was a scarce item or needed to complete a set.

As with so many sports or hobbies, the terminology has built up over the years and can cause problems for the inexperienced. If it was possible to turn the clock back and establish a grading system for card condition it is most unlikely that words like 'good' or 'fair' would be utilised. But whatever grading system might be used there will always be differences of opinion, even between reasonable and well-meaning people, as to the condition of any particular card. Not surprisingly, these differences most often occur when one person is selling and another is buying.

A few years ago, and after pressure from some of the members, the Cartophilic Society bravely produced a recommended grading guide. With the Society's permission this is reproduced on page 146. Probably wisely, they did not opt for a clean break with established terminology but endeavoured to define some of the terms that had built up by use over the previous 60 or

more years. They settled on five grades ranging from 'excellent' as top condition through 'very good', 'good' and 'fair' to the bottom rating of 'poor'. Even so, a number of auctioneers, dealers and advertisers still use other terms such as 'finest collectable condition' to indicate the top grade and variations such as 'near mint', 'good to very good' or 'very poor' to define lower grades.

This may seem pedantic but it is important because the value of a particular card rests, amongst other things, on its condition. So even if you are quite happy to collect cards that are worn or damaged you will want to make sure you buy them at a discount to the undamaged price. The problem is exacerbated when auctioneers and dealers have to apply a description to a set of cards. The prospective purchaser would expect all cards in a set described as 'very good' to meet this description. The seller, however, might take the view that a couple of cards with minor blemishes would not alter the general rating of the set, especially if they were the end cards which are always subject to more wear.

At the end of the day there is no substitute for experience and, whilst most dealers are very fair in exchanging cards or refunding money if the customer is dissatisfied, the old dictum of 'let the buyer beware' should be borne in mind.

COLLECTING

Bidding at auction and purchasing from dealers are the most common ways to acquire cards today. Of course, collecting from packets of tea, cigars or other commodities and swopping with like-minded collectors to complete sets, is still a very satisfying activity. There is also the possibility that relatives or friends may find in their attic a collection of previously forgotten cards and donate these to you. But if you want a good representative collection, or are pursuing a particular theme, then at some point cards have to be purchased.

If you have access to transport then cards can be inspected and purchased at a wide range of auctions, card fairs or club meetings which are held at many different locations throughout the British Isles. If transport is difficult then all of

Player's Cigarettes.

COLDSTREAM GUARDS.

Player's Cigarettes.

16th LANCERS.

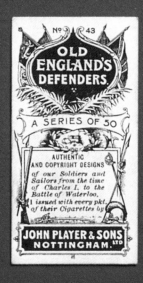

Player's Cigarettes.

3rd DRAGOON GUARDS.

Player's Cigarettes.

ROYAL SCOTS.
(LOTHIAN REGT.)

Player's Cigarettes.

KING'S OWN
SCOTTISH BORDERERS.

GRENADIER GUARDS.

"BLENHEIM" "RAMILLIES"
"OUDENARDE" "MALPLAQUET"
"DETTINGEN" "LINCELLES"
"CORUNNA" "BARROSA"
"PENINSULA" "WATERLOO"
"ALMA" "INKERMAN"
"SEVASTOPOL"
"EGYPT 1882" "TEL-EL-KEBIR"
"SUAKIN 1885"
"KHARTOUM"
"SOUTH AFRICA"
1899

JOHN PLAYER & SONS, LTD
CASTLE
TOBACCO FACTORY,
NOTTINGHAM.

Nº 27 MILITARY SERIES OF 50 REGIMENTS

Nº 43

OLD
ENGLAND'S
DEFENDERS.

A SERIES OF 50

AUTHENTIC
AND COPYRIGHT DESIGNS
of our Soldiers and
Sailors from the time
of Charles I. to the
Battle of Waterloo,
I issued with every pkt.
of their Cigarettes by

JOHN PLAYER & SONS
NOTTINGHAM. LTD

Royal Artillery. 1807.

Piper

78TH Highlanders 1814

Royal
Horse Guards
Blue 1807

A.B. Seaman 1805

Admiral 1805.

PLAYER'S CIGARETTES.

1914 STAR & BAR.
GT BRITAIN.

British Medals (Series 2)
& Decorations, No 8.

Egypt. 1801.

Red Eagle. Prussia.

MITCHELL'S CIGARETTES.

SOUTH AFRICA, 1877-9.

WILLS'S CIGARETTES

A PURITAN WOMAN ABOUT 1640

PLAYER'S CIGARETTES

A YOUNG GALLANT OF 1640-50

A Gentleman
of the reign of William IV

G. RICHARDS

Turn over & Spot the Winner

No. 1 OF A SERIES OF 50.

OGDEN'S CIGARETTES

GORDON RICHARDS

GORDON RICHARDS

HAS HE THE RECORD
FOR MOST WINS IN A DAY?

GORDON RICHARDS

the major, and many of the smaller, dealers have mail order facilities, and postal bidders are well catered for by the organisers of specialist card auctions. Read the small print of any sales lists or catalogues, however, to make sure you know what your rights are regarding items that do not meet the advertised description. In most cases returns are allowed and refunds granted provided the item is promptly sent back with an adequate reason for rejection.

Anyone seriously interested in collecting cards should join a club, which gives the opportunity, not just to meet a wide range of fellow collectors, but also to participate in club auctions, where cards can frequently be acquired at a fraction of catalogue prices. Joining the Cartophilic Society of Great Britain is another firm recommendation, as, for a modest annual subscription, members receive an excellent bi-monthly magazine, regular postal auction lists, access to approval book rounds, the use of a comprehensive library and the ability to purchase reference books at a discount. The work carried out by the Society on research is truly staggering but despite the hundreds of thousands of cards covered by the reference books new discoveries occur regularly. The real possibility of finding a new card or variety is one of the attractions of cartophily.

As well as reference books, all collectors will need to obtain one or more of the priced sales lists – usually referred to as catalogues – published by the major dealers. These are generally issued annually and establish prices for the forthcoming calendar year. The London Cigarette Card Company has been publishing catalogues since 1929 and claims to have the largest stock of cigarette cards in the world. Murray Cards (International) Ltd publishes a single volume covering both cigarette and trade cards, which is widely used by others in the trade as their main point of reference to current values. Another well distributed catalogue is Albert's *Guide to Cigarette Card Collecting* but this does not quote prices for odd cards or cover trade cards.

These catalogues not only give prices but also illustrate cards and provide a good deal of helpful information to both the novice and experienced collector. Value Added Tax is chargeable on cards and the catalogues referred to above all show prices inclusive of VAT. Each vendor has his own individual terms of sale so these need to be checked and compared as well as the prices. Note, also, that end cards in a set are priced at a premium to normal cards, as primitive storage methods used in the past have made them scarcer.

All three of the publishers have retail outlets at which cards can be inspected and purchased but the main purpose of the catalogues is to generate mail order sales. There are many other dealers who produce price lists and it is always worth subscribing to a selection of these. But when even the largest dealers do not have the item you want in stock or may be charging too high a price for your budget, you might then turn to the auction houses.

AUCTIONS

A few words of advice on buying at public auctions, especially for the uninitiated. Always study the auction catalogue beforehand, mark the items that interest you and make sure the auctioneer's terms and conditions are understood. View the lots you wish to bid for and make sure they are as described. Do not be afraid to open boxes or take sets of cards out of their wrappers to inspect them but be extremely careful and replace the lots as you find them. Many items, especially those of higher value, are sold in plastic pages which enables viewing to take place without handling the cards. Decide in advance the maximum sum you are prepared to pay for each lot and stick to it. Never bid for items you have not viewed even though they seem to be selling very cheaply.

Most skilled auctioneers knock down lots at between 120 and 200 per hour so events move fast. Scratching your ear or blowing your nose will not attract a bid but waving to a friend might! If you wish to bid make it clear to the auctioneer and drop out as soon as the bidding exceeds your limit.

Auctions are a good place to buy scarce cards, part sets and also the more common sets. Collectors use them to dispose of unwanted cards and dealers find them useful to shift stock

page 20
Three popular themes

Left to right

Top row: Medals and Decorations
Player **War Decorations & Medals**, 1927 (G, set of 90)
Taddy **British Medals & Decorations**, c1912 (C, per card)
Allen & Ginter **The World's Decorations**, c1890 (C, per card)
Mitchell **Medals***, 1916 (J, set of 25)

Middle row: Costumes
Wills **English Period Costumes**, 1929 (G, set of 50)
Player **Dandies**, 1932 (D, set of 50)
Carreras **British Costumes**, 1927 (F, set of 25)
Brooke Bond **British Costume**, 1967 (B, set of 50)

Bottom row: Jockeys
Phillips **Sportsmen – Spot the Winner***, (inverted back) 1937 (F, set of 50)
Ogden's **Champions of 1936**, 1937 (H, set of 50)
Phillips **In the Public Eye**, 1935 (D, set of 54)
Ardath **Sports Champions**, 1935 (G, set of 50)

which is not readily marketable. Bargains are often secured but if two determined bidders want a scarce item then catalogue value can easily be exceeded. For details of auctions, card fairs, club meetings and, indeed, anything cartophilic, a subscription to *Card Times* is excellent value. This is an independent magazine that is published eleven times each year specifically for cigarette and trade card collectors. The London Cigarette Card Company publishes a monthly magazine, *Cigarette Card News And Trade Card Chronicle* and, again, this is well worth the subscription price. Although it

does not contain advertisements it does include a free type card and lists of special offers.

STORAGE

Having acquired cards the next problem is how to store them. The advent of plastic pages and loose leaf albums has considerably improved the options available. The prime objective is to keep the cards free from damage in such a way that they can be viewed easily. Plastic pages meet this criteria but they do have some disadvantages. They cannot cope with all shapes and sizes nor can they satisfactorily display horizontal and vertical designs within the same set. They are also bulky to store and can be costly for those with large collections. The old 'slip-in' albums used before the war have the same disadvantages and 'corner-slot' albums, although cheaper, should be avoided as in time they damage the cards.

Corner mounting in scrap books or photograph albums allows more scope for artistic layout but does mean the backs of the cards cannot easily be viewed. The use of the type of photo album with clear pages that adhere to the backing page should be avoided except, perhaps, for silks. These have no wording on the back and can be mounted on thin card to prevent the adhesive from damaging the fabric. Cards lend themselves admirably to being mounted and framed but really this is for decoration and is not a practical storage system. Those with the necessary skills can construct their own albums combining the best of each system but for most people the convenience and safety of the plastic page will be the most desirable solution.

Never glue cards into an album, never store in a damp place and avoid putting rubber bands round cards to keep them in place. If albums are found to be too bulky or expensive then cards can be wrapped in pieces of paper and stored neatly in a drawer or a cardboard box. But if you do this, make sure you have a good index system so that you can find a particular card or set when required.

Cards can be indexed and stored by subject, by maker or category of issuer, by year or period of issue or by a combination of these. For

Magazines and reference books are invaluable to collectors

example, a subject basis may be used but with separate sections for cigarette cards issued at home, those issued overseas and for trade cards. Another possibility is to index by issuer but split into chronological sections covering the periods before the Great War, between the wars and post-war. Subject collecting is probably the most popular but can cause problems where a set of cards covers many different topics.

SELLING

The day may come when you wish to dispose of some or all of your cards. This may be the result of an ongoing policy to buy collections and then sell those items surplus to requirements, because collecting interests have changed, or perhaps some unexpected bills arrive and liquid assets become the priority. Sadly, selling is never as easy as buying and the results can be painful, especially if cash is needed in a hurry.

Basically, the same methods are available for selling as for buying but whereas catalogues give a good indication of the price you have to pay for an item, there is no similar market indicator when you come to sell. You can advertise your cards at a certain price or put them in an auction with a reserve but there is no certainty that they will sell. A dealer will always have a significant margin between his selling and buying prices to cover overheads, finance charges and, quite reasonably, profit. The margin widens for common cards and for cards in grubby or damaged condition. This is because these cards do not have such a ready market and may have to be kept in stock for much longer periods.

A set of cards in the mid-price range, say F to H in the *Price Guide Index*, ought to sell for around 40% to 50% of catalogue value if in 'excellent' or 'very good' condition. But this will depend on whether the dealer you approach needs that set or already has an adequate stock, whether at auction two or more people decide to bid for it or whether, if advertised, the person who would be willing to pay your price

actually sees the advertisement. Whilst you might well get a higher price by advertising or selling through an auction you will also have additional costs and will have to wait longer for your money. Auction commissions are generally between 10% and 15% plus, if appropriate, VAT. Members of the Cartophilic Society can, however, place 'memberads' in the *Cartophilic Notes & News* magazine free of charge.

The more common sets, cards in a lesser condition or stuck into albums and even severely damaged rare cards have a very limited market. On the other hand, scarce items in very good condition are always wanted, as are cards on popular subjects such as golf and cricket. Certain makers are especially sought after such as Taddy and F & J Smith. Those who wish to collect with investment potential in mind would be wise to stick to the classic early cards and smaller manufacturers unless they have the time to analyse which categories of cards might be undervalued and thus ripe for an upward movement in price.

Special albums with cards stuck-in are attractive but have little value

Wills **Radio Celebrities** (1st Series), and **Wild Flowers 2nd Series** stuck in their special albums (B, per album)

OGDEN'S CIGARETTES.

DAVID LIVINGSTONE.

Honours & Ribbons Nº 17.

Victoria Cross. (Army.)

WILL'S CIGARETTES.

MOSCOW.

THE FINISH

WHOSE DIMPLES AND LAUGHING EYES ARE THESE?

ELISSA LANDI FOX

CAPT PERCY SCOTT.

LAMBERT & BUTLER'S CIGARETTES

"London Characters"—
THE CORNET PLAYER

PLAYER'S CIGARETTES

THE ROBIN

CHURCHMAN'S CIGARETTES

KING HENRY VII MAKING
OBEISANCE BEFORE THE ALTAR

CHAPTER 3

PRINTING AND PRODUCTION

The enjoyment of card collecting can be much enhanced by acquiring some knowledge of how the cards were produced and the methods used by the printing firms. After examining a few dozen cards from each of the different eras of production, it will be seen that there is a wide variety of styles and methods of presentation. The most obvious distinctions are between monochrome and colour and between printed and photographic cards. Other variations might simply be the different styles used by the artists or the reproduction methods utilised by the printer.

Cards that have been printed have generally been produced by one of three methods – letterpress, lithography or photogravure. Other processes, such as collotype, were used but on a very limited basis. Printing is a complex process and it is not the intention here to explain these methods in great detail but rather to give a very general overview. In essence, the above three processes transfer ink onto the card from a raised surface, a flat surface and a sunken surface respectively.

LETTERPRESS

The majority of cigarette cards were printed by the letterpress process, especially the output between the wars. The simplest form we can find on cards is one colour line work. B Morris & Sons used this process for their series of HOW TO SKETCH. The design is first photographed and chemical processes are then used to etch this on to the printing plate. The resulting design stands proud and when the raised metal is inked it prints the card. Two or more colours can be used by etching additional plates and printing them one after the other in different inks. Millhoff's THINGS TO MAKE is a good example of two colour line work.

Millhoff **Things To Make**, 1935 (F, set of 50)

WILLS'S CIGARETTES

SIR HENRY WOOD

WILLS'S CIGARETTES

SULLIVAN.

When enlarged, the three main methods of printing can be distinguished more easily

Above left:
Letterpress – Wills **Radio Celebrities** (1st Series), 1934

Middle:
Lithography – Wills **Musical Celebrities** (1st series), 1912

Right:
Photogravure – Hill **Famous Cricketers**, 1923

Letterpress printing, a comparison of the use of black ink and violet tinted brown ink

Left: Churchman **East Suffolk Churches**, 1912 (I, set of 50)

Right: Churchman **Kings of Speed**, 1939 (F, set of 50)

The half-tone process is a more complicated form of letterpress printing which gives a much more satisfactory result. The method is similar to line work except that at the outset a screen is placed between the artwork and the camera. This screen is made of glass with a very fine network of criss-cross lines running through it. The photographic plate, therefore, depicts the design as a series of dots and it is these dots that are etched onto the printing plate. The fineness of the printing depends on the number of dots to the inch, which in the case of cigarette cards, can be up to 150 to the inch.

An example of half-tone printing using one colour is Churchman's EAST SUFFOLK CHURCHES where black ink was used. If the colour of the ink is changed a different effect is achieved, as is the case when the same issuer used tinted brown ink to produce KINGS OF SPEED. As with line work, more than one colour can be used by etching additional plates and one of the miracles of the printer's art is the ability to match any number of colours in the artist's original work by using just three plates.

This is achieved by creating all the colours from the three primary colours of yellow, red and blue. At the photographic stage colour filters are used which firstly, only allow yellow onto the plate, then the process is repeated with a separate plate for red and for the final plate a

CHURCHMAN'S CIGARETTES

HASKETON.

CHURCHMAN'S CIGARETTES

J. A. MOLLISON

filter excludes all but the colour blue. For each photograph the glass screen is moved slightly so that the dots for each colour will have a different alignment and will not print one on top of the other.

Although three plates are all that are needed to match any hue or shade, an additional plate is generally prepared in black which has the effect of strengthening the picture and, if necessary, printing a border. LONDON CHARACTERS from Lambert & Butler is an example of the three colour process whereas BRITISH BUTTERFLIES from Godfrey Phillips uses four colours. The half-tone process can be combined with line work and Player's TENNIS is a good example. The foreground figures are printed from half-tone blocks and the green background and sketched figures are line work. Sometimes an additional varnishing process is used which almost gives the impression of a photographic card. Ardath's FAMOUS FILM STARS and FAMOUS FOOTBALLERS have been treated in this way.

The backs, other than for some early cards, are also generally printed by letterpress with the type set mechanically on a linotype machine. One colour is normal but two colours can sometimes be found. The backs are worth more than the casual glance they get from many collectors. The headings and the layout of the text usually work well but on occasions are messy or featureless.

The ornamental designs on the early issues are a true delight and it is clear that a great deal of time and thought was spent by the compilers on preparing the reverse of the card.

LITHOGRAPHY

The Greek translation of this process means literally, 'written on stone'. This was, indeed, the method in early lithography as the design was drawn by wax crayon on smooth limestone. After damping, a greasy ink was applied to the surface of the stone and the ink adhered to the crayon drawing but was repelled by the damp stone. When paper was applied to the stone the drawing appeared in reverse. To obtain a drawing the right way round the early artists had, of necessity, to put their design directly on to the stone in reverse.

Unlike letterpress, colour, or chromo-lithography, cannot be made up successfully from just the three primary colours. A colour print had to be built up by adding a succession of tints and each of these tints required a separate stone. Often up to 12 stones would be required and the original design would have to be copied on to each stone by skilled litho-

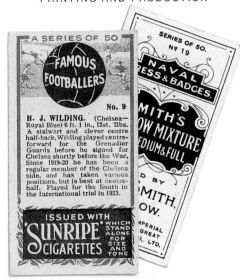

Backs are normally printed in one colour and only rarely in two

Hill **Famous Footballers**, 1923 – back in brown and green (I, set of 50)
Smith **Naval Dress & Badges**, 1914 – back in blue (C, per card)

Player **Tennis**, 1936 (F, set of 50), printed by letterpress using line work and half-tone blocks

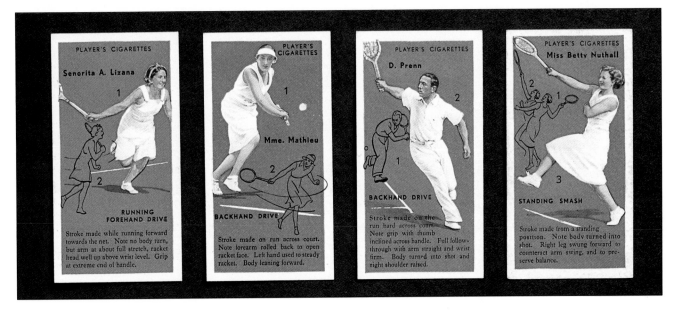

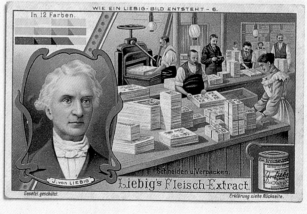

This set illustrates the build-up of colours in lithography

Liebig (F 849) **Production of a Liebig Card**, 1906 (E, set of 6 extra large)

artists. An attractive set of six cards from the firm of Liebig, numbered 849 in the *Fada* catalogue, details the production of a lithographed series of cards. An inset portrait also shows how the tones are built up by successive colour printings. It was the German printing firms who first perfected chromo-lithography and many of the British and American cards produced during the Victorian period were printed in Germany.

Many excellent examples of good quality lithographed cards can be found, including Player's WONDERS OF THE DEEP and Wills' THE WORLD'S DREADNOUGHTS. But it will be apparent from the description of the process given above that lithography was cumbersome and time consuming. The first improvement came with the replacement of natural stone by thin metal plates, usually made of zinc or aluminium. This led to the introduction of the offset press in 1908, which enabled printing to take place on continuously revolving cylinders, rather than flat-bed presses. The development of photo-lithography enabled designs to be transferred on to the stone or plate photographically.

Although some examples can be found among the other tobacco houses, Gallaher were the firm to make the most significant use of the offset rotary machine. FILM PARTNERS, GARDEN FLOWERS and WILD ANIMALS are three examples and these cards were probably printed using up to eight colours. Modern trade cards are commonly produced using offset litho although generally only four colours are used – yellow, red, blue and black.

PHOTOGRAVURE

Gravure, or recess printing, resembles etching in that the design is actually sunk into the plate. The artwork is first photographed and colour filtered in a similar way to the letterpress process but, in this case, it is the design itself which etches into the printing plate. Ink is applied to the face of the plate and then wiped off so that only the recessed areas retain ink. The plate is brought into contact with the card, which has been slightly dampened, and the ink is absorbed by the card.

The darker the colour of the original the deeper the recesses and, therefore, the greater the amount of ink retained and then transferred to the card. Because of the nature of the process, the 'dots' representing the design tend to blur into each other thus giving a softer and richer result. For some reason this process was not too popular but Edwards, Ringer & Bigg's ALPINE VIEWS, Hill's THE RAILWAY CENTENARY and CINEMA STARS from Richard Lloyd are worth looking for. Cope's CASTLES is another example but in this case a glossy overprinting has been applied to give a shiny finish. The SPECIAL JUBILEE YEAR SERIES, printed by Bemrose and Son for Godfrey Phillips, is available at modest cost and shows a rare usage of the three colour gravure process.

PHOTOGRAPHIC CARDS

These were briefly popular around the turn of the century with Ogden's in particular making good use of the process for their GUINEA GOLD* cards. In the middle of the 1930s they became fashionable again and many manufacturers issued 'real' photographic cards with the firms of Ardath and Pattreiouex much to the fore.

Offset lithography was widely used by Gallaher in the 1930s
Gallaher **Film Partners**, 1935 (F, set of 48)

Richard Lloyd **Cinema Stars**, 1937 (G, set of 25), printed by photogravure

GLAMIS CASTLE

HARLECH CASTLE

NEWQUAY

KYLE OF LOCHALSH

Hand coloured real
photographs
Top row:
Hill **Views of Interest,
Second Series**, 1938
(C, set of 48 large)

Bottom row:
Hill **Views of Interest, Third
Series**, 1939
(C, set of 48 large)

The subject matter for the cards is
photographed and the negatives mounted on a
glass plate. Where a caption is to appear on the
face of the card a small portion of the film is
removed and the titles are separately photographed to be added later. Prepared paper is
continuously fed beneath the negatives as they
are exposed to light. The prints are then
developed, rinsed, fixed and washed and,
depending on the effect required, they might
also be chemically toned.

Some photographic series, such as Hill's VIEWS
OF INTEREST were also coloured by hand. The
tinting was applied through stencils and in the
case of the Hill's series five colours were used,
all of which required separate stencils. Quick
drying tints would have been brushed onto the
cards through the apertures in the stencils. It is
not uncommon to find colours overlapping due
to badly cut or wrongly positioned stencils.

Some superb photographic series were
prepared with outstanding clarity, such as
Pattreiouex's BRITISH RAILWAYS and COASTWISE,
but the cards do have a tendency to curl and
many collectors are not over keen on them for
this reason.

Above: Pattreiouex **British Railways**, 1938 (F, set of 48 medium). *Below*: **Coastwise**, 1939 (C, set of 48 medium)

THE PRINTING HOUSES

As noted in the section on lithography, many of the early cards issued in the UK were printed in Germany. Wills' CRICKETER SERIES 1901 and the earlier 1896 series were both printed by Meissener & Buch of Leipzig. Paris also had a good reputation for high class colour printing and Wills' SOLDIERS OF THE WORLD* was printed there by the firm of Champenois.

Wills with their huge sales could afford to commission their own individual series of cards but in the 1890s there were many tobacco companies of lesser size who, perhaps, only needed a print run of 100,000 cards. The firm of A Hildesheimer & Co were the main agents who co-ordinated the printing requirements for several of the smaller companies. Thus the manufacturer who required a small quantity of cards would end up paying a cost per 1,000 based on a much larger print run. It was, of course, a fairly inexpensive matter to put the name of the sponsor and an advertisement on the back, as these would be printed in a single colour. For some even this was too costly and the cards were issued with plain backs and, therefore, became anonymous once removed from the cigarette packet.

With the requirement for more individuality, coupled with the growing sales of cigarettes during the Edwardian period, the practice of shared issues gradually faded out. It is worth noting, however, that as late as 1916 a series of

WAR PORTRAITS was printed by Forman of Nottingham, which is estimated to have been utilised by around 50 different trading concerns.

Before the introduction of the cigarette card, the tobacco manufacturers had established business relations with printing firms for stationery and packaging. The well known house of Mardon, Son & Hall can trace their association with the tobacco industry back to 1846, when they printed wrappers for Franklyn & Co of Bristol. Mardon were to become much more closely involved with their other neighbours, W D & H O Wills, who first ordered boxes from them for their growing cigarette trade around 1883.

By 1897 Mardon's art department employed around two dozen people who would have been actively designing packets and show cards as well as cigarette cards. Two years on and the firm became one of the first in Europe to acquire a rotary printing press using aluminium plates. As descriptive texts on the reverse of cards became standard Mardon built up an editorial department and a reference library which eventually numbered over 5,000 books.

In 1902 they became a key acquisition of the Imperial Tobacco Company and were formed into the Printing & Packaging Branch. In this capacity they printed countless millions of cards and were responsible for the design, artwork and copy for most of them. Sadly, the staff artists were not allowed to sign their work so the bulk of their output remains unattributed. Mardon also carried out printing work for BAT who in 1962 took a 50% interest in the business and a few years later acquired complete control.

Another Bristol-based printing firm who played an important role in card production was E S & A Robinson. Wills used them for their 1899 issue of SEASIDE RESORTS and Carreras and Taddy were among other tobacco firms to utilise their services. But Robinson are probably best remembered for their excellent offset litho work

Ogden's **Guinea Gold***, (numbered 201-500) c1900 (A, per card)

Wills **Kings and Queens***, 1902 (B, per card) printed by Mardon, Son & Hall

Wills **Seaside Resorts**, 1899 (C, per card) printed by Robinson

Gallaher **Woodland Trees**, 1912 (B, per card) printed by Thos Forman & Sons

page 33
Some early lithographed series were printed in Paris.
Wills **Soldiers of the World***, 1895 (C, per card)

for Gallaher in the 1930s. Tillotsons of Bolton and Liverpool were another major printer of packaging and cards. They did some early work for Ogden's, including printing many of the TABS* series, and produced cards for Gallaher and other manufacturers either side of the Great War. They were also important printers of silk inserts.

Thos Forman & Sons printed many cigarette and trade cards and among the best were the two sets of WOODLAND TREES and BIRDS, NESTS & EGGS for Gallaher. From time to time they also helped out their Nottingham neighbours, John Player & Sons, including the attractive 1924

issue of DRUM BANNERS & CAP BADGES.

Bemrose and Son of Derby became quite substantial printers of cards during the 1930s, producing many series for the Godfrey Phillips group of companies and also for Carreras and Ardath. Examples of their work from 1935 for the latter company include SILVER JUBILEE and SPORTS CHAMPIONS.

Many other printers were, of course, involved in the design and production of cards and some of these are recorded in the reference books. Sadly, there are dozens of firms whose work we can admire today but whose names are never likely to be known.

INDIA.

Bengal Lancers.

INDIA.

Bombay Lancers.

INDIA.

Lifeguards.

INDIA.

Madras Light Cavalry.

JAPAN.

Artillery.   Marching order.

JAPAN.

General.   Full dress.

JAPAN.

Horse-guard.   Full dress.

JAPAN.

Infantry of the Guards.
Marching order.

ROUMANIA.

Non-Commissioned Officer.
Chasseurs.

NORWAY.

Royal Guards.

MOROCO.

Soldier.

ITALY.

Gunner Horse Artillery.

Player **Characters from Fiction**, 1933 (G, set of 25 large) from artist H M Brock

page 35, top to bottom
Left row: artist Arthur Wardle. Player **Dogs** (full length), 1933 (G, set of 25 large)
Right row: artist Roland Green. Player **Game Birds & Wild Fowl**, 1928 (H, set of 25 large)

Spy (Leslie Ward) was the artist responsible for many of the cartoons which appeared in *Vanity Fair* magazine. Wills '**Vanity Fair**' **Series** (unnumbered), 1902 (B, per card)

THE ARTISTS

Modern productions from, among others, Imperial Tobacco and Brooke Bond readily give credit to the artists and writers who have created a series of cards. Before the 1939/45 war the general view was that where the design was the work of a printing firm's art department, or even an agency, it was a team effort and, therefore, should not be signed. This policy has denied card lovers and researchers the opportunity of giving proper recognition to a large number of extremely talented people.

Fortunately, this policy did not usually apply where outside artists and illustrators were commissioned. True, some of this work was 'borrowed' in that it was originally created for other purposes than a cigarette card. George Studdy's 'BONZO' DOGS series for John Player and the Spy (Leslie Ward) cartoons which featured in Wills' 'VANITY FAIR' SERIES are two such instances. Many original works were also commissioned and John Player were among the more active in this respect.

Christopher Clark, one of the leading historical painters of the day, was an ideal choice for Player's DANDIES, while H M Brock, whose illustrations grace many fine books, did an excellent job with the artwork for two series of GILBERT AND SULLIVAN plus CHARACTERS FROM

FICTION. For their several series of dogs issued between 1925 and 1933, Player chose the gifted animal painter, Arthur Wardle, and the same artist also produced a colourful set of 50 DOGS for Wills in 1937. The well-known bird artist, Roland Green, produced some very realistic paintings for GAME BIRDS & WILD FOWL, which look especially good in the large series of

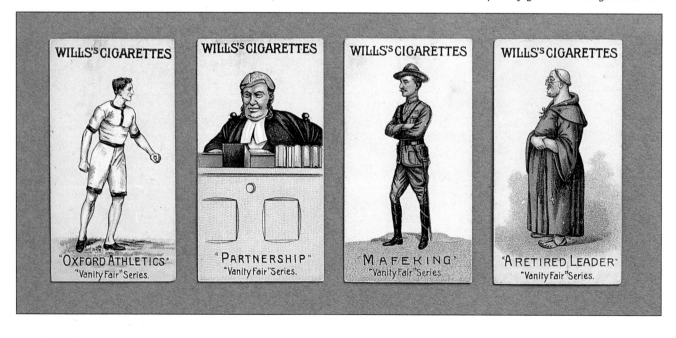

PLAYER'S CIGARETTES

WELSH SPRINGER SPANIEL.

PLAYER'S CIGARETTES.

WILD DUCK·OR MALLARD.

PLAYER'S CIGARETTES

WIRE-HAIRED FOX TERRIER

PLAYER'S CIGARETTES

MONGOLIAN PHEASANT.

25. Peter Scott, the naturalist, artist and son of explorer Captain Scott, prepared the artwork from which the 1937 series of WILDFOWL was produced.

Player also employed many caricaturists with excellent results. 'Mac' (Douglas Machin) and 'Rip' (R P Hill) both produced a series of 50 footballers and in addition 'Rip' also drew Player's first between-the-wars set of cricketers in 1926. This included a superb sketch of J M Gregory, the Australian fast bowler, hurling down one of his express deliveries. The set also included a poignant likeness of Roy Kilner, who was to die two years later of enteric fever. A most amazing series of STRAIGHT LINE CARICATURES was another issue in 1926, this time from the pen of Alick Ritchie.

Ritchie also produced a most delightful set of 50 cards for Ogden's under the title of SHOTS FROM THE FILMS. Here we can find Eleanor Powell, Buddy and Vilma Ebsen tripping the light fantastic from 'Broadway Melody of 1936' and Charles Laughton and Clark Gable at loggerheads in 'Mutiny On The Bounty'. Ogden's used another of the caricaturists previously featured by Player when they issued their FOOTBALL CARICATURES in 1935. The artist was, of course, 'Mac' and a close look at his signature on the front of the cards reveals that the artwork was dated 1931. It is interesting to speculate what had happened to it in the intervening years.

Ogden's featured soccer and rugby

Player **Cricketers, Caricatures by 'Rip'**, 1926 (H, set of 50)

PLAYER'S CIGARETTES.

Mr. J M GREGORY N·S·W AUSTRALIA

PLAYER'S CIGARETTES.

R KILNER YORKSHIRE

Brilliant caricatures from 'Mel', 'Mac' and Alick Ritchie

Left to right:
Top row, first and second cards: Churchman **Men of the Moment in Sport**, 1928 (J, set of 50)
Top row, third and fourth cards: Churchman **Sporting Celebrities**, 1931 (I, set of 50)

Bottom row, first and second cards: Ogden's **Football Caricatures**, 1935 (I, set of 50)
Bottom row, third and fourth cards: Ogden's **Shots from the Films**, 1936 (H, set of 50)

Look the other way when the girl at the tea house smiles.

·A hollow building echoes all sounds; a vacant mind is open to all suggestions.

Colourful work by René Bull.
Churchman **Eastern Proverbs 2nd Series**, 1933
(D, set of 12 large)
Churchman **Eastern Proverbs 3rd Series**, 1933
(C, set of 12 large)

league players in their caricatures, but Wills' set of RUGBY INTERNATIONALS by 'Mel' consisted wholly of players from the union code. 'Mel' was the signature used by J B Melhuish, who was also active between 1928 and 1931 on behalf of Churchman's. He produced two series for them, MEN OF THE MOMENT IN SPORT and SPORTING CELEBRITIES. In the latter set he depicts the British Middleweight Champion, Len Harvey, with an impish grin on his face whilst the American Ryder Cup Captain, Walter Hagen, juts out his lower lip as he contemplates an iron shot onto the green.

Other artists worth looking out for are Julius M Price, who drew the 80 LONDON TYPES for Carreras, Will Owen whose MORE LEA'S SMOKERS for R J Lea are absolute gems and Peter Fraser, who is guaranteed to make you chuckle with his HUMOROUS DRAWINGS. These were distributed by Stephen Mitchell in 1924. Another whose colourful portrayals are superbly executed is René Bull who produced EASTERN PROVERBS and HOWLERS for Churchman. Finally, compare the contrasting styles of Joseph Clayton Clark, or 'Kyd' as he signed himself, in his portrayals of CHARACTERS FROM DICKENS for Player and VOTARIES OF THE WEED for Gallaher.

Player's Cigarettes.

Mr Bumble.   Oliver Twist.

Gallaher's Cigarettes.

Left: Player **Characters from Dickens** (1st Series), 1912
(G, set of 25)
Right: Gallaher **Votaries of the Weed**, 1916 (B, per card)

WILL'S CIGARETTES

Mrs Brandt.

WILL'S CIGARETTES

TURKISH SABRE-HILT.

CABUL, 1842 (AFGHANISTAN).

WILL'S CIGARETTES

WILL'S CIGARETTES

SCHOOL ARMS.
ELTHAM COLLEGE.
THE ROYAL NAVAL SCHOOL.

ESTO PERPETUA

WILL'S CIGARETTES.

FELUCCA.

WILL'S CIGARETTES.

BRITISH GUIANA.

WILL'S CIGARETTES.

EVOLUTION OF A STAR.

CASTELLA CIGARS

Robert Stephenson & Hawthorn 0-6-0T

WILL'S CIGARETTES

W. BOYES (WEST BROMWICH ALBION)

CHAPTER 4

THE ITC GIANTS

Of all the series of cigarette cards attributed to British manufacturers in the reference books and catalogues, three firms on their own account for over 25%. They are W D & H O Wills of Bristol, John Player & Sons of Nottingham and Ogden's Limited of Liverpool. They formed the backbone of the Imperial Tobacco Company (ITC) from 1902 until cigarette cards ceased to be issued in 1940. Each of these firms has its own interesting history and they all enjoyed relative independence in their marketing and card issuing policies after amalgamation in 1902.

W D & H O WILLS

As noted earlier, Wills was the dominant member of the ITC and are thought to be the first British firm to make use of cigarette cards. These early cards, produced in the normal small card size, were used to promote the various tobacco products sold by the company. The first is believed to have been issued in 1887 or 1888 with around twenty different cards following during the next six years. Coincidentally, 1888 was also the year in which the enduring Wild Woodbine brand of cigarettes was launched.

The founder of the firm was Henry Overton Wills, who as a young man of 25, established a tobacco business in Bristol in 1786. When he died 40 years later, his two sons, William Day and Henry Overton the Second, took over the management of what had become a thriving concern. Strangely, both brothers were reputed to be non-smokers.

In 1893 the firm became incorporated with the name W D & H O Wills Limited and, as noted in Chapter 1, became a founder member of, and was absorbed by, the Imperial Tobacco Company. These changes in corporate structure are important to collectors as the company name printed on the cards can materially assist in establishing dates of issue. For example, any card issued for the home market from 1902 onwards should indicate that Wills was a branch of the Imperial Tobacco Company. This statement is referred to as the 'ITC Clause', and should also appear on cards issued after 1902 by other ITC branches.

Quite possibly, Wills issued cards of actresses and beauties with their export brands prior to 1893, as these have been found showing the firm's name without the addition of 'Limited'. It is, however, fairly certain that their first series of cards for the home market appeared in 1895 and that this was a set of 25 SHIPS* featuring naval vessels. The series was subsequently extended to 100 cards by including a selection of passenger liners and foreign vessels. Also in

Mr Henry Overton Wills (1761-1826), founder of W D & H O Wills

The first Wills cards were reproductions of their show-cards.

Wills **Advertisement Cards***, c1893 (K, per card)

---

page 38

Wills, *top to bottom*

Left row:
Actresses* (Grey scroll back), c1897 (D, per card)
School Arms, 1906 (F, set of 50)
Romance of the Heavens, 1928 (D, set of 50)

Middle row: **Nelson Series**, 1905 (J, set of 50)
Gems of French Architecture, 1917 (G, set of 50)
Rigs of Ships, 1929 (H, set of 25 large)
In Search of Steam, 1992 (E, set of 30 large)

Right row:
Medals*, c1905 (J, set of 50)
Flags of the Empire 2nd Series, 1929 (E, set of 25)
Association Footballers, 1935 (G, set of 50)

Wills **Ships*** (Three Castles back),1895 (F, per card)

Wills **Cricketers,1896***, 1896 (G, per card)

1895 a series of 50 cards depicting SOLDIERS AND SAILORS* and a further issue of 100 SOLDIERS OF THE WORLD* were being inserted in domestic packs of Wills' cigarettes.

A change of direction in subject matter was made in 1896 when a series of 50 CRICKETERS, 1896* was issued. Most of the leading players of the period were shown in attractive head and shoulder portraits. W G Grace had broken several batting records the previous season, including 1,000 runs in May, and was naturally included. A C MacLaren was another record breaker with a score of 424 against Somerset in 1895, while Richardson, the Surrey fast bowler,

was included, following his success in capturing 290 wickets during the 1895 season.

To coincide with Queen Victoria's Jubilee in 1897 a series of 50 KINGS AND QUEENS* was produced and in the next few years a variety of interesting sets followed, including DOUBLE MEANING*, SEASIDE RESORTS and SPORTS OF ALL NATIONS. These early issues rarely had any descriptive matter on the reverse of the card, which often consisted simply of ornamental scrollwork. KINGS AND QUEENS* was an exception but unfortunately the compiler made a number of errors, including details given on the card depicting Queen Victoria, which had to be replaced. This somewhat ill-fated series was re-issued in 1902 for King Edward's Coronation with four of the original cards deleted and five new subjects, including the Prince and Princess of Wales, added.

A very attractive CORONATION SERIES of 60 cards was also issued about this time but, as was so often the case with these early cards, there are at least two varieties to collect. The design on the back of the cards incorporated two small arrows and in one printing they are 'wide' and in another they are 'narrow'.

Wills was in trouble again with another contemporary issue of 'VANITY FAIR' caricatures. The cards proved popular so a second series of

50 was issued, including on card 29, the Archbishop of Canterbury. It is believed that the primate objected to the wording but, whatever the problem, the card was withdrawn and replaced. So, there are 51 cards to look out for in this particular series. Another interesting point about this set is that it included the Chairman of the ITC, Sir William Henry Wills, who is referred to as 'Birdseye'.

LOCOMOTIVE ENGINES AND ROLLING STOCK* can be collected both with and without the ITC Clause. Whether the cards were originally intended for export, or whether they were printed before Imperial Tobacco was formally constituted, is not known for certain. The set of 50 cards without the clause has an additional complication in that seven of the subjects were replaced after the first printing by more modern locomotives. These problems fade into insignificance, however, compared to the many reprinted and replacement cards that can be found in the TRANSVAAL SERIES distributed at the time of the Boer War.

After 1902 a more consistent pattern began to emerge, in the main due to the design and printing work being transferred to Mardon, Son & Hall. The confusion over which cards were distributed in the home and export markets also diminished, with BAT taking over responsibility

Sir William Wills, first Chairman of the ITC, as pictured in Wills 'Vanity Fair' Series (unnumbered), 1902 (B, per card)

Left: Backs of Wills' cards with and without the ITC Clause

Right: Wills **Coronation Series**, 1902 with backs showing wide and narrow arrows, (B, per card)

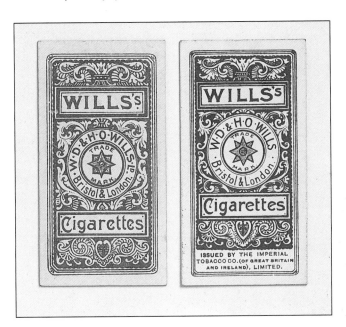

Wills **Locomotive Engines and Rolling Stock***, 1901
(C, per card)

Wills **Borough Arms***,
(unnumbered) 1904
(G, set of 50)

Wills **Aviation**, 1910
(H, set of 50)

for sales outside Great Britain and Ireland. It should be noted, however, that neither the *World Index*, nor the main priced catalogues, show these overseas issues under the section for BAT cards. It is considered less confusing to collectors to list export issues under the name of the appropriate ITC branch whose name actually appears on the card.

Some splendid series were put out during the years leading up to the First World War. A feature of this period is the many heraldic sets produced, particularly the long running series of BOROUGH ARMS*. Another subject treated most sympathetically by Wills over the years was flowering plants. OLD ENGLISH GARDEN FLOWERS and ROSES both ran to two series of 50 and ALPINE FLOWERS to one. The naval theme was revived in 1905 with a NELSON SERIES followed four years later by NAVAL DRESS & BADGES. In 1910 Wills achieved a notable 'first' by issuing a set of 50 cards on the subject of AVIATION.

A fine set of MUSICAL CELEBRITIES was issued in 1912 but when in 1916 a second series was produced it caused an outcry. The compilers had included eight personalities of German or Austrian origin and the 'offending' cards were quickly replaced and the originals destroyed. Those that survived are exceedingly scarce and expensive. Another casualty of the war was a series of 50 cards which Wills had planned to issue in 1915 to mark the centenary of the Battle of Waterloo. At the last minute the Directors decided to abort the distribution of the cards on the grounds that they might offend our French allies. Only a few sets escaped being pulped and these are, understandably, highly prized.

The support received from Canada and Australia during the War was recognised with two series of cards – OVERSEAS DOMINIONS (CANADA) and OVERSEAS DOMINIONS (AUSTRALIA). Our European Allies were remembered with three sets featuring the famous buildings and architecture of Belgium, France and Russia. A similar Italian series was prepared but not

issued. More obvious as weapons of propaganda were the twelve cards of RECRUITING POSTERS, a series of 50 MILITARY MOTORS and in March 1917 a set of ALLIED ARMY LEADERS. As well as being superbly printed, this issue has some curiosity value in that it was prepared before the capitulation of Russia and the entry of the United States into the War.

Another unusual feature of this period was the activity of the Press Bureau. The set of MILITARY MOTORS can be collected with a statement on the front 'Passed for Publication by the Press Bureau 21.9.16' and also without. Despite giving a fair amount of information about our military capability of the time the Censor was seemingly happy as no changes were made between the first and second printings. ALLIED ARMY LEADERS is another issue that carries the Press Bureau endorsement. By the end of 1917 all production of cigarette cards had ceased and it was to be another five years before they would reappear.

In September 1922 smokers were pleasantly surprised to find packed with their Gold Flake cigarettes a series of DO YOU KNOW. Wills followed this up in 1923 with 50 GARDENING HINTS and a very attractive set of WILD FLOWERS. This latter set can be collected with or without two small black dots in the top panels on the reverse of the card. The reason for these 'secret marks' has never been satisfactorily explained. One theory was that they were put there to distinguish between two different printings. The

---

page 43

A selection of Wills flower cards

Left to right, top row:
Alpine Flowers, 1913 (G, set of 50)
Roses (1st Series), 1912 (G, set of 50)
Roses 2nd Series, 1914 (G, set of 50)
Old English Garden Flowers (1st Series), 1910 (F, set of 50)

Middle row:
Flowering Shrubs, 1935 (F, set of 30 large)
Flower Culture in Pots, 1925 (E, set of 50)
Garden Flowers New Varieties 2nd Series, 1939 (E, set of 40 large)

Bottom row:
Wild Flowers, 1923 (E, set of 50)
Do You Know 4th Series, 1933 (D, set of 50)
Garden Flowers, 1933 (E, set of 50)
Wild Flowers (1st Series), 1936 (D, set of 50)

WILL'S CIGARETTES.

ALPINE TOADFLAX.

WILL'S CIGARETTES.

Amy Robsart.

WILL'S CIGARETTES.

Corallina.

WILL'S CIGARETTES.

HONEYSUCKLE.

WILL'S CIGARETTES

SHRUBBY MAGNOLIA

WILL'S CIGARETTES.

GLOXINIA.

WILL'S CIGARETTES

GERBERA (Transvaal Daisy)   Variety: JAMESONII HYBRIDS

WILL'S CIGARETTES.

PRIMROSE.

WILL'S CIGARETTES.

FUCHSIA AND DAHLIA.

WILL'S CIGARETTES.

TEN-WEEK STOCKS.

WILL'S CIGARETTES

BLUEBELL

Wills **Do You Know 4th Series**, 1933, (D, set of 50)

page 45
A selection of large cards from Wills

Top to bottom, left row:
Heraldic Signs & Their Origin, 1925 (G, set of 25)
Famous Golfers, 1930 (D, per card)
Modern Architecture, 1931 (G, set of 25)

Right row:
Old Silver, 1924 (G, set of 25)
Lawn Tennis, 1931, 1931 (J, set of 25)
Modern Architecture, 1931 (G, set of 25)

'do you know' format proved very popular at the time with a further three series being produced over a ten-year period. There is a nice touch in the 4th series with an illuminated Wills' sign and the 'Star' trademark appearing on card no. 35.

The inter-war years were truly a golden age as far as collectors were concerned. Wills had now largely switched to the more modern letterpress printing method and for quantity and variety of interest no other British manufacturer could equal them. Even during the coupon war of the early 1930s Wills continued to issue cards, although, with the emphasis on the sectional series of famous paintings, this was perhaps the low point of the period. Sectional series, consisting of large pictures divided into card-sized portions, were difficult to display, and to this day do not appeal to many collectors.

Among the finest of Wills' productions were the large cards inserted in packs of 50 and 100 cigarettes. In terms of numbers printed they are very much scarcer than the standard sized cards but for many years they were overlooked by the majority of collectors. Even today, they are extremely good value despite the fact that growing demand has caused prices to increase quite rapidly.

HERALDIC SIGNS & THEIR ORIGIN from 1925 is a must for any collector with an interest in the subject of heraldry. BRITISH SCHOOL OF PAINTING, MODERN BRITISH SCULPTURE, OLD POTTERY & PORCELAIN and OLD SILVER are sets that will delight the connoisseur and amateur antique collector alike. One of the best series of this genre is MODERN ARCHITECTURE with pictures of Broadcasting House, Liberty's, Selfridge's and County Hall from London, and Nottingham and Belfast represented by The Council House and the Parliament Building respectively. The compilers of the series did not forget their home city of Bristol and show the University Tower which was opened by the King in 1925. The magnificent tower was funded by the Wills family in memory of Henry Overton Wills.

The somewhat up-market image of the large card issues was maintained with Wills' sporting issues. A set of GOLFING was distributed in 1924 and a lovely set of 25 FAMOUS GOLFERS appeared

F. J. PERRY

Wills **British Sporting Personalities**, 1937 (F, set of 48 medium)

in 1930. In the last few years the demand for anything golf-related has helped push the price of these sets beyond the pocket of many collectors. Not that the series on LAWN TENNIS issued in 1931 has lagged that far behind in interest and value. It features 25 of the leading players of the pre-war period including the popular British stars, 'Bunny' Austin and Betty Nuthall. Fred Perry was not included and had to wait for recognition until Wills issued their set of BRITISH SPORTING PERSONALITIES with Embassy cigarettes in 1937.

The standard sized cards covered the most popular sports of the day, namely, cricket and football. Two sets of each were issued, the cricketers being particularly well produced. This was a fairly meagre output compared to some of the other tobacco houses and the same situation can be noted with film stars. Wills issued two sets of 25 CINEMA STARS in 1928 and a third of 50 in 1931, and that was it. Set after set of portraits of footballers or film stars was not their scene. The wireless, as a result of the policies of Lord Reith, had a more classy image, and was rewarded with two series of 50 RADIO CELEBRITIES in 1934 and 1935. Not that

WILLS'S CIGARETTES.

E ROSE.

WILLS'S CIGARETTES.

MUSTARD-POT.

WILLS'S CIGARETTES.

ROGER H. WETHERED.

Wills's Cigarettes

H. W. Austin

Wills's Cigarettes

The County Hall, London

Wills's Cigarettes

Parliament Building, Belfast

Above

Left to right, first and second cards:
Wills **Cricketers, 1928**, 1928 (H, set of 50)

Third and fourth cards:
Wills **Cinema Stars 1st Series**, 1928 (G, set of 25)

Below

Left to right, top row:
Wills **Gardening Hints**, 1923 (C, set of 50)

Bottom row:
Wills **Household Hints**, 1936 (C, set of 50)

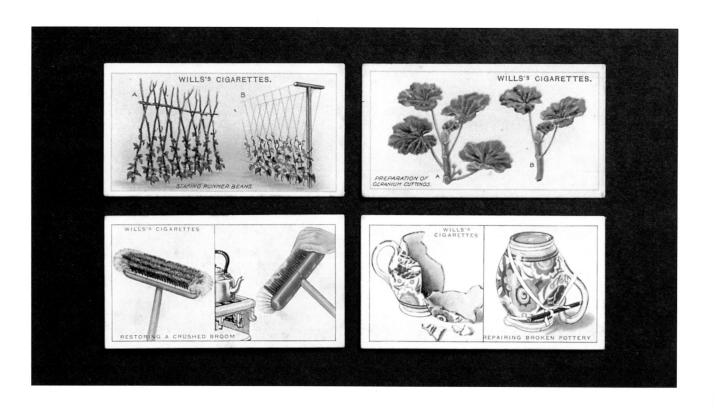

popular artistes were overlooked, with Gracie Fields and 'Stainless Stephen' rubbing shoulders with Stuart Hibberd and Sir Henry Wood.

The gardener and the householder were well served with the issue of several sets of flowers interspersed with HOUSEHOLD HINTS, GARDENING HINTS and GARDEN HINTS. The latter items must have been invaluable at a time when most families could not afford books or magazines. Today, however, it seems rather quaint to read about how to whitewash a ceiling or how to restore a crushed broom. Some tips, such as repairing cracks in cement, are, however, as useful now as they were in the 1930s.

Transport was another of Wills' inter-war specialities. Four series of 50 cards featured the railways with RAILWAY LOCOMOTIVES from 1930 being, perhaps, the most attractive. Mention must be made, however, of RAILWAY EQUIPMENT which is chock full of interesting information. SAFETY FIRST is the only series dealing with motoring but it is a fascinating production full of period gems such as, 'do not give incorrect hand signals' and for the cyclist, 'beware of tram lines'. STRANGE CRAFT was an unusual series put out in 1931 and included details of a concrete ship and a steam submarine. But on the sea this was the age of the passenger liner. MERCHANT SHIPS OF THE WORLD from 1924 pictured the Aquitania, the Mauretania and the huge Majestic. Ten years on and some new generation vessels mingled with the old in two magnificent series of 30 large cards titled FAMOUS BRITISH LINERS. The passenger liner survived for some years after the war – sadly, the cigarette card did not.

In 1981, however, the name of Wills was once again to be found on the back of a set of picture cards – not packed with cigarettes but with Embassy cigars. The first series of 36 medium sized cards called WORLD OF SPEED was reminiscent of the 1938 production of SPEED. The cards, if a little thinner than before, were excellently designed and printed. Card no. 33 pictured the powerboat Uno Embassy and provided just a little extra promotion for Wills' products. Further series followed and currently cards are being packed with the Castella brand of cigars. The popularity and demand for these well-designed and colourful issues can be gauged by the prices they realise at auctions.

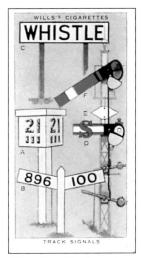

Wills **Railway Equipment**, 1939 (C, set of 50)

Left to right

Top row:
Wills **Railway Locomotives**, 1930 (H, set of 50)

Bottom row:
Wills **Strange Craft**, 1931 (G, set of 50)

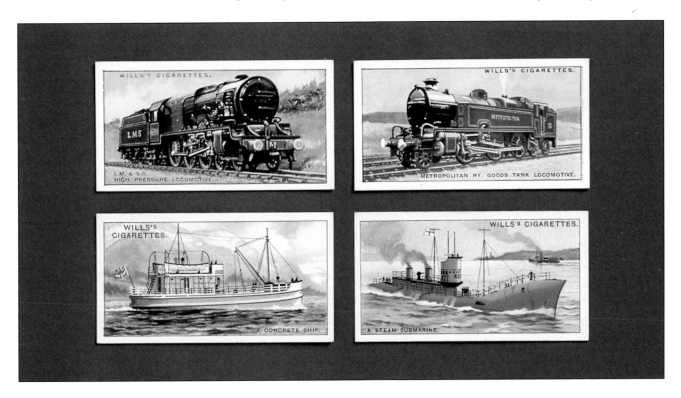

John Player (1839-1884), founder of John Player & Sons

Player **Actors and Actresses***, 1898 (E, per card)

Top right

Above: Player **Wild Animals of the World** (narrow), 1902 (B, per card)

Below: Player **Wild Animals of the World** (normal), 1902 (A, per card)

JOHN PLAYER & SONS

In 1862 when John Player arrived in Nottingham from his home in Saffron Waldon it was to take up a job as a draper's assistant. He soon set up his own establishment selling agricultural fertilisers and seeds as well as developing a useful sideline in supplying his customers with tobacco. This 'sideline' soon proved to be the more profitable venture and so in 1877 Player purchased a tobacco factory belonging to William Wright. Expansion swiftly followed and in 1881 the site at Radford was acquired and the Castle Tobacco Factory constructed. The first trademark was an illustration of Nottingham Castle and this appeared on the back of some of the early card issues. The founder died in 1884 and management of the firm eventually passed to his two sons, J D and W G Player. The famous 'Sailor's Head' framed within a lifebuoy was registered as a trademark in 1891.

As with W D & H O Wills, the first cards Player issued are thought to be advertisements for the firm's tobacco products and date from 1893-94. The first series proper may have been a set of 20 CASTLES, ABBEYS ETC IN THE UNITED KINGDOM which can be collected with two styles of printing. No indication is given on these cards that Player had become a limited company in 1895, so the series may date from that year or even earlier. In the years prior to their merger into the Imperial Tobacco Company Player issued some fine series, including sets of 25 ACTORS AND ACTRESSES*, 50 ACTRESSES*, 50 CITIES OF THE WORLD and 20 FAMOUS AUTHORS AND POETS*.

The first of many superb naval and military series was ENGLAND'S NAVAL HEROES which appeared as a set of 25 about 1897. A second series with descriptive backs followed and with the Boer War on the horizon a set of 25 ENGLAND'S MILITARY HEROES was distributed. These cards, plus FAMOUS AUTHORS AND POETS* and WILD ANIMALS OF THE WORLD, can be collected in standard size and also in a narrow 28mm size. The official explanation was that these cards were printed for insertion into packets of 12 Gold Leaf cigarettes, but it is possible that the narrow size, about the width of

Dingo.

Puma.

three cigarettes, was to fit much smaller packets or even for insertion with one ounce packets of tobacco.

Two other classics of the period are OLD ENGLAND'S DEFENDERS and MILITARY SERIES. BADGES & FLAGS OF BRITISH REGIMENTS was produced after the formation of the ITC, as was REGIMENTAL COLOURS AND CAP BADGES*. Sets of 50 of these cards were produced for both the regular and territorial regiments. The territorial regiment set and the early badges and flags set can be collected with different coloured backs. Having mentioned the backs, these really are worth a second look as they are miniature works of art in their own right. CELEBRATED BRIDGES is another lovely early set and the BRITISH EMPIRE SERIES shows many fascinating scenes from around the world.

page 49

Player, *top to bottom*

Left row:
Advertisement Cards*, c1894 (K, per card)
Picturesque London, 1931 (H, set of 25 large)
History of Naval Dress, 1930 (G, set of 50)

Middle row:
Celebrated Bridges, 1903 (J, set of 50)
Cities of the World, c1900 (K, set of 50)
Famous MG Marques, 1981 (D, set of 28 large)

Right row:
Gallery of Beauty, c1896 (E, per card)
British Regalia, 1937 (F, set of 25 large)
RAF Badges (with motto), 1937 (F, set of 50)

PLAYER'S NAVY CUT CIGARETTE TOBACCO

PLAYER'S CIGARETTES

Player's Cigarettes.

Gallery of Beauty No. 7.

CITIES OF THE WORLD   No. 46. BUENOS AYRES

The Lake, St. James's Park.

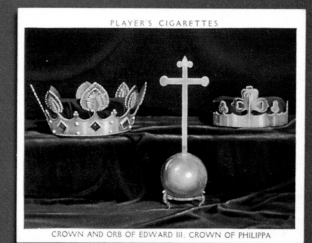

PLAYER'S CIGARETTES

CROWN AND ORB OF EDWARD III. CROWN OF PHILIPPA

PLAYER'S CIGARETTES.

OFFICER, 1740.

MG 260

PLAYER'S CIGARETTES

No. II (BOMBER) SQUADRON, R.A.F.

Player was to show a distinct literary bias over the years and among the more unusual items, from about 1904 or 1905, was a series of 12 bookmarks with an inset photo of many of the popular authors of the day. Among others we can find Kipling, Conan Doyle and Lord Tennyson. The art nouveau style decoration on the front of these cards is superb. 1905 was the centenary of Trafalgar and the death of Lord Nelson. Player's LIFE ON BOARD A MAN OF WAR marked these events by comparing the activities of sailors in 1805 and 1905. BUTTERFLIES & MOTHS, FISHES OF THE WORLD and USEFUL PLANTS & FRUITS were other contemporary series of distinct merit. As with so many sets of this time, neither of the latter two were numbered.

A year or two later Player started on an interesting run of three series known as COUNTRY SEATS AND ARMS*. On card no.146 in the third series they depicted the residence of Lord Winterstoke, The Chairman of The Imperial Tobacco Company. The noble Lord was, of course, none other than Sir William Wills, who had been elevated to the peerage in 1906. He remained chairman of the ITC until his death at the age of 80 in 1911. A lovely NATURE SERIES was issued in 1909 as was the much copied ARMS & ARMOUR set. A series of 25 CEREMONIAL AND COURT DRESS appeared in 1911, no doubt with the Coronation of King George V in mind. CHARACTERS FROM DICKENS in two series of 25 and a further 25 CHARACTERS FROM THACKERAY were among the cards issued as the war clouds gathered in the years leading up to1914.

Player's 1914 issues included a set of 25 called the VICTORIA CROSS and 10 extra large cards featuring ALLIED CAVALRY. A set of 25 on NAPOLEON the following year would have been issued with our French allies in mind and the Empire was not forgotten with COLONIAL & INDIAN ARMY BADGES. POLAR EXPLORATION ran to two series of 25 and, apart from the subject matter, they are interesting for the different design styles adopted for the backs. The first series used the floral, ornamental style typical of the pre-war period, whereas the second series with its plain, austere look, characterised the inter-war years.

The first items issued after the suspension of cards in 1917 were reprints of pre-war series. The two series of CHARACTERS FROM DICKENS were reissued as a set of 50 in November 1923 and even new series, such as DRUM BANNERS & CAP BADGES and ARMY, CORPS & DIVISIONAL SIGNS, had a pre-war feel to them. Then in December 1925 a set of 50 GILBERT AND SULLIVAN cards was issued, based on paintings by H M Brock. This signalled a new approach with a number of well known artists and caricaturists being commissioned to design fresh and original card series (see pp 34–35).

For the next few years Player produced cards which were as good as, if not better, than those of any other manufacturer. Many of these sets were printed on plain white card, without a

Player **Bookmark Photographs***, 1905 (G, per card)

The home of Lord Winterstoke, Chairman of the ITC

Player **Country Seats and Arms Third Series***, 1907 (F, set of 50)

Player **Gilbert and Sullivan**,
1926
(H, set of 25 extra large)

Player

Left to right, top row:
Poultry, 1931 (G, set of 50)

Left to right, bottom row:
Derby and Grand National Winners, 1933 (H, set of 50)

frame line, in striking colours. Each also had a concise and well-written text on the reverse. MILITARY HEAD-DRESS, POULTRY, BUTTERFLIES, DERBY AND GRAND NATIONAL WINNERS and AVIARY

AND CAGE BIRDS are among the sets that should be represented in every collection. There were many fine large card series put out between the wars and some, like the unique and superb series of CATS, adopted the same format as described above. For CHARACTERS FROM FICTION Player again employed the talent of H M Brock, but the artists responsible for the subtle but beautiful series of PICTURESQUE BRIDGES and PICTURESQUE LONDON remain anonymous.

The 'sticky back' era effectively started in 1934. Player's series of 50 FILM STARS was among the first to suffer this treatment but, although serious collectors hated them, the public at large found the concept of an adhesive back and a special album extremely useful. The subject matter also found favour and a second series quickly followed, with a third making its appearance in 1938. Although the 150 cards are a fine record of the stars of the period, the artwork compared unfavourably with, for example, the contemporary issue of CRICKETERS, 1934. Cricket was a consistent theme of Player's, a set of 50 cards appearing every four years from 1926 onwards. Football was also popular with five series between 1926 and 1930 followed by HINTS ON ASSOCIATION FOOTBALL in 1934. This series and the 1930 production of

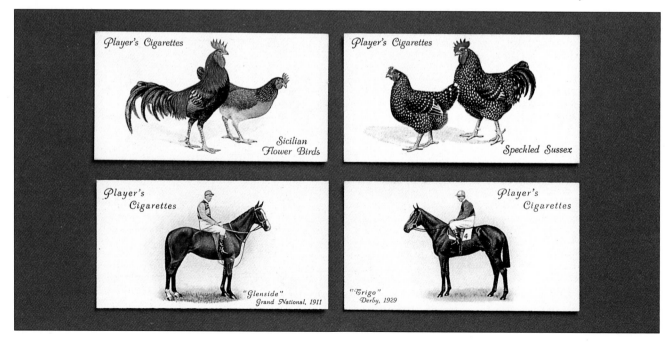

ASSOCIATION CUP WINNERS are exceptional both for style and content.

Many of the minority sports were acquiring a larger following and Player was quick to recognise this. TENNIS and SPEEDWAY RIDERS, which appeared in 1936 and 1937 respectively, were two such activities. Like Wills, Player reserved their golfing sets for the large cards packed with boxes of cigarettes. Motor travel was becoming more common and with air travel constantly in the news it is not surprising that these subjects proved popular. The sets featuring MOTOR CARS, AEROPLANES (CIVIL) and INTERNATIONAL AIR LINERS were particularly well produced.

From 1938 the threat of war influenced subject matter, with AIRCRAFT OF THE ROYAL AIR FORCE, MODERN NAVAL CRAFT and UNIFORMS OF THE TERRITORIAL ARMY all being issued in standard sized sets of 50. This latter series is interesting in that, being issued after war had been declared, a second printing had to be made to alter some of the wording. Another surprising fact is that card no.17 actually depicts the then Chairman of the Imperial Tobacco Company. A few non-military items were distributed as well, perhaps the best being a striking set of ANIMALS OF THE COUNTRYSIDE and a previously overlooked subject, CYCLING.

After the War it was a long wait until 1975 when Player started packing THE GOLDEN AGE OF MOTORING with their Doncella cigars. The adhesive back was dispensed with but excellent albums were made available free so that collectors could insert the cards with corner mounts if they so wished. Cards on steam, flying and sail followed and the early 1980s saw a number of excellent series produced on Britain's flora and fauna. At this time cards were also being distributed with Grandee and Tom Thumb cigars, the latter including some especially fine sets on the HISTORY OF MOTOR RACING, HISTORY OF BRITAIN'S RAILWAYS and HISTORY OF BRITISH AVIATION.

Player **Association Cup Winners**, 1930 (H, set of 50)

Above:
Player **Cricketers, 1934**, 1934(G, set of 50)

Left:
Player **Hints on Association Football**, 1934 (D, set of 50)

2 ♥ ♥ ♥

OGDEN'S CIGARETTES.

Time of Victoria. 1875.

Loading a 15 pounder Field Gun.

Ogden's Guinea Gold Cigarettes.

OGDEN'S CIGARETTES.

"THE POETRY OF MOTION."

OGDEN'S CIGARETTES.

RUBY-CROWNED KINGLET.

OGDEN'S CIGARETTES.

ROYAL CINQUE PORTS YACHT CLUB.

OGDEN'S CIGARETTES

HAND STAND DIVE

BRITISH BIRDS' EGGS   OGDEN'S
TREE-PIPIT   49   CIGARETTES.

OGDEN'S CIGARETTES.

"PLYMOUTH LTD" EXPRESS, G.W.R.

OGDEN'S CIGARETTES

H. LARWOOD

OGDEN'S

The founder of the business, Thomas Ogden, established a tobacconist's shop in Park Lane, Liverpool in 1860. Within a short time other branches were opened across the city and in 1866 a manufacturing base was set up in St James' Street. Rapid expansion followed, until in the 1890s the firm was operating from six different factories and warehouses. Incorporation had taken place in 1890 but a few months later Thomas Ogden died, leaving as his legacy one of the largest and most successful firms in the tobacco industry.

There was an obvious need to consolidate the company's business within one location and in 1899 construction was started on a huge complex in Liverpool's Boundary Lane. The factory was opened in 1901 with the capacity for manufacturing a colossal 900 million cigarettes per annum. The commitment and exposure to such rapid expansion was a contributory factor in Ogden's swift capitulation to James B Duke, when the American tycoon made his offer to buy out the business.

The growth of Ogden's was due, in part at least, to their extensive advertising and to the use of cards. The famous photographic cards, inserted with a new brand of Guinea Gold cigarettes dating from 1894, proved an instant success. Although photography had been around for many years, it was only in the 1890s that modern shutters and coated films helped stimulate the growth of amateur photography.

Photographic cards had already been used in North America and may also have influenced Ogden's to use this medium.

No firm record exists as to which were the first GUINEA GOLD* cards issued but they were probably unnumbered, plain backed cards, featuring actors and actresses. Numbered cards of celebrities were first distributed in 1900 or 1901 at about the time of the Tobacco War. A special album was advertised to hold the cards and a scheme for purchasing filled albums for a guinea was instituted. The cards were issued for a continuous period of 13 years and it has been estimated that, counting all the lettering, caption and portrait variations, it would be possible to collect 20,000 different pictures.

Another major success for Ogden's was the introduction of their Tabs brand at five for 1d (one old penny) at around the turn of the century. The cards packed with these cigarettes were not the glossy photos given away with Guinea Golds but had black and white fronts printed by letterpress. The most commonly found are the various GENERAL INTEREST series which contained pictures of actors, actresses, celebrities, military leaders, sportsmen, warships, castles, animals and events. Diverse subjects, such as 'The Human Ostrich' and '25,000 Battersea School Children Parading Before Princess Louise', abound in these GENERAL INTEREST series.

Conventional standard sized cards were also put out, both before and during the Tobacco War, but mainly of the ubiquitous beauties of the period. Some of these cards are, however, superbly printed and those with a playing card inset on the front are thought to have been packed in export brands only. Providing some variety was an attractive set of 48 VICTORIA CROSS HEROES and this included two of the leading Generals engaged in the Boer War, Sir Redvers Buller and Lord Roberts. A striking SHAKESPEARE SERIES*, which exists both numbered and unnumbered, also dates from about this period. Once Ogden's were firmly entrenched as part of the Imperial Tobacco Company, a wide variety of excellent series were issued, fully up to the standard of the best from Wills and John Player.

Ogden's **Fowls Pigeons & Dogs**, 1904 (J, set of 50)

---

page 54, Ogden's, *top to bottom*

Left row:
Beauties* (playing card inset), c1899 (F, per card)
Marvels of Motion, 1928 (G, set of 25)
Swimming, Diving and Life-Saving, 1931 (G, set of 50)

Middle row:
Beauties* (coloured, green net back), 1901 (E, per card)
Guinea Gold* (Boer War base D), c1900 (A, per large card)
Foreign Birds, 1924 (G, set of 50)
Birds' Eggs, 1904 (I, set of 50)
Records of the World, 1908 (G, set of 25)

Right row:
British Costume from 100BC to 1904, 1905 (B, per card)
Club Badges, 1914 (B, per card)
Champions of 1936, 1937 (H, set of 50)

Ogden's

Left to right, top row:
Guinea Gold* (numbered 1-200), c1900 (H, set of 200)
Guinea Gold* (numbered 201-500), c1901 (A, per card)
Guinea Gold* (numbered 201-500), c1901 (A, per card)

Bottom row:
Tabs **General Interest*** (E Series), c1901 (I, set of 120)
Tabs **General Interest*** (F Series), c1901 (A, per card)
Tabs **General Interest*** (A Series), c1901 (I, set of 150)

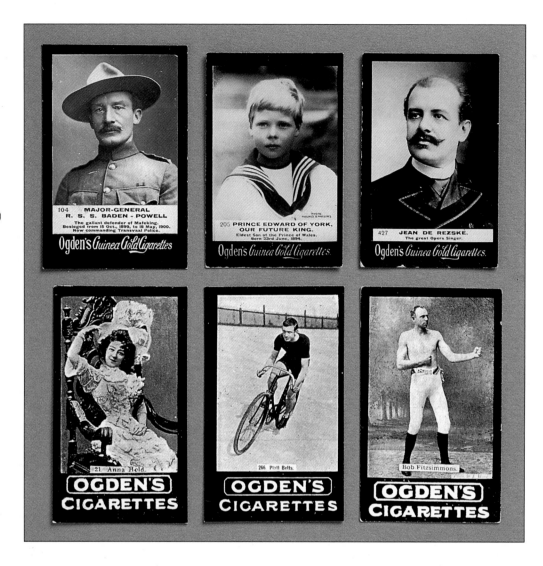

page 57, left to right

Ogden's

Top row, first and fourth cards:
Victoria Cross Heroes, c1901 (C, per card)

Top row, second and third cards:
British Birds, 1905 (H, set of 50)

Middle row, first and second cards:
Beauties 'HOL'*, c1898 (D, per card)

Middle row, third and fourth cards:
Owners Racing Colours & Jockeys, 1906 (J, set of 50)

Bottom row, first and second cards:
Flags & Funnels of Leading Steamship Lines, 1906 (K, set of 50)

Bottom row, third and fourth cards:
Orders of Chivalry, 1907 (J, set of 50)

FOWLS PIGEONS & DOGS from 1904 was an interesting composite set much copied by other members of the ITC group. Another early production was BRITISH COSTUMES FROM 100 BC TO 1904, a well-conceived set of 50 which sadly lacks any descriptive text. OWNERS RACING COLOURS & JOCKEYS is another with no text but the back is so superbly designed it scarcely matters. A delightful set of 50, richly coloured on the front and with an informative text, was the series of FLAGS & FUNNELS OF LEADING STEAMSHIP LINES.

One of the notable features of Ogden's pre-1914 cards, apart from the obvious quality of production, is the interest of the subject matter.

Even today, the topics covered have hardly been overdone. Some popular themes were attempted and with FOOTBALL CLUB COLOURS and FAMOUS FOOTBALLERS, two series of BRITISH BIRDS, ORDERS OF CHIVALRY and PUGILISTS & WRESTLERS it can be seen that there was enough variety to keep everyone happy. In 1908 Lord Baden-Powell founded the Scout movement and in the period between 1911 and 1914 Ogden's issued no less than five sets of cards on the subject. Pitching tent, tracking, signalling – even how to hold pets – all featured among the 225 cards.

With the advent of war, sets covering INFANTRY TRAINING and MODERN WAR WEAPONS were issued, both somewhat austere with

BRITISH BIRDS.
19 BULLFINCH.

OGDEN'S CIGARETTES

BRITISH BIRDS.
35 GUILLEMOT.

OGDEN'S CIGARETTES

OGDEN'S

WORLD FAMED

CIGARETTES

TRADE MARK

LIVERPOOL

ENGLAND.

OGDEN'S CIGARETTES.

E. WHEATLEY

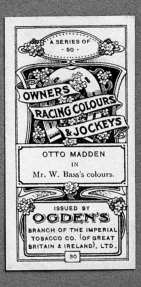

A SERIES OF 50

OWNERS RACING COLOURS & JOCKEYS

OTTO MADDEN
IN
Mr. W. Bass's colours.

ISSUED BY
OGDEN'S
BRANCH OF THE IMPERIAL
TOBACCO CO. (OF GREAT
BRITAIN & IRELAND), LTD.

30

Ogden's Cigarettes.

**BRITISH INDIA
STEAM NAVIGATION
COMPANY, LTD.,
LONDON.**
House Flag & Funnel.

Ogden's Cigarettes.

**CANADIAN
PACIFIC
RAILWAY CO.,
MONTREAL.**
House Flag & Funnel.

OGDEN'S CIGARETTES.

BADGE.
KNT. COMMANDER OF THE BATH.
(MILITARY.)

OGDEN'S CIGARETTES.

BADGE.
ORDER OF MERIT.
(NAVAL AND MILITARY.)

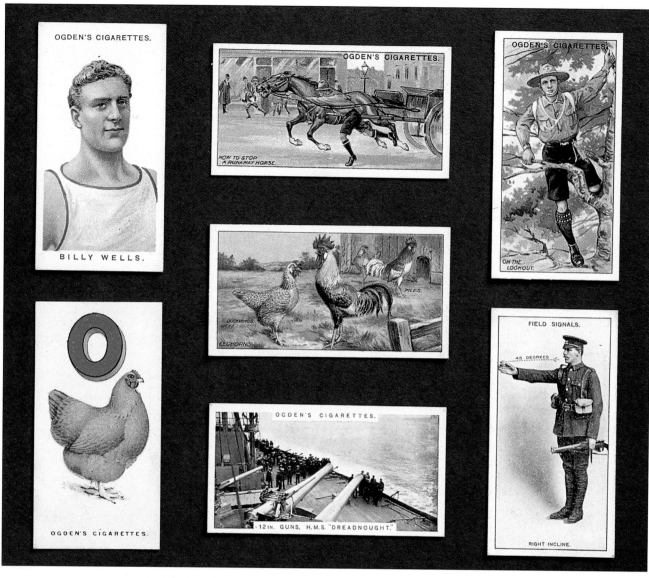

Ogden's, *top to bottom*

Left row:
Boxers, 1915 (B, per card)
Poultry Alphabet, 1924 (G, set of 25)

Middle row:
Boy Scouts 2nd Series, (blue back), 1912 (J, set of 50)
Poultry 2nd Series, 1916 (H, set of 25)
Modern War Weapons, 1915 (J, set of 50)

Right row:
Boy Scouts (1st Series, blue back), 1911 (J, set of 50)
Infantry Training, 1915 (I, set of 50)

monochrome fronts. Interestingly, two series of 25 POULTRY were also distributed in 1915 which, if nothing else, reinforce the view that Ogden's were one of the great innovators of the period. The domestic fowl theme continued with the resumption of card issues after the Great War when in 1922 the first of two series of 25 POULTRY REARING & MANAGEMENT was issued.

The next few years were heavily dominated by cards featuring various sports, especially horse racing. Quite a few of the sets were printed in brown or sepia which can give a somewhat monotonous effect when mounted in

albums. Cricketers, footballers, rugby players, boxers and even 'dirt-track' riders were all allocated individual sets but for devotees of the turf there were no less than ten different series in the period up to 1931. TRAINERS, AND OWNERS' COLOURS 1st and 2nd series from 1925/26 and DERBY ENTRANTS, 1926 are among the best of these sets and would certainly enhance any collection.

In 1930 the Hignett Brothers branch was merged into Ogden's and from that date any cards put out by Hignett were identical to Ogden's issues other than for the name of the manufacturer. Coincidentally, at about this time the card issuing policy seemed to change, as the series became more varied and the cards looked more vibrant and colourful.

CONSTRUCTION OF RAILWAY TRAINS from 1930, MOTOR RACES, 1931 the following year and BY THE ROADSIDE issued in 1932 were all welcome variations on themes that had been used by other manufacturers. The set of 50 RACING PIGEONS, the striking production of AFC NICKNAMES and the stimulating STORY OF SAND confirmed that the art of innovation had not been lost.

By 1936 the cinema and film stars were very hackneyed themes, yet Ogden's in their SHOTS FROM THE FILMS made a bold and successful attempt to try something different. Similarly, ACTORS, NATURAL & CHARACTER STUDIES looked at film and stage actors from a new and stimulating angle. For the 1937 Coronation of King George VI a sectional set was issued and, although these were generally unpopular with collectors, this series succeeded brilliantly as each card was a picture in its own right. BROADCASTING, FOOTBALL CLUB CAPTAINS, HOW TO SWIM, OCEAN GREYHOUNDS and PICTURESQUE VILLAGES kept up Ogden's reputation for quality.

AIR-RAID PRECAUTIONS from 1938, also issued by Wills and others in the ITC group, was the beginning of the end for Ogden's as a card issuer. Two superb sets, BRITISH BIRDS & THEIR EGGS and SEA ADVENTURE were distributed in 1939 and these brought down the curtain so far as cards were concerned. In 1962 cigarette manufacturing ceased and today the Ogden's name is associated only with the manufacture and sale of pipe tobacco.

Ogden's **Famous Dirt-Track Riders**, 1929 (H, set of 25)

Ogden's **Actors, Natural & Character Studies**, 1938 (G, set of 50)

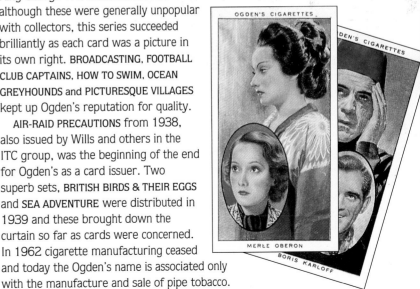

ADKIN'S CIGARETTES.

AN AUSTRALIAN MOTH & LARVA.

ADKIN'S CIGARETTES.

BRIMSTONE BUTTERFLY & LARVA.

FAULKNER'S CIGARETTES

OPTICAL ILLUSION. No. 9.

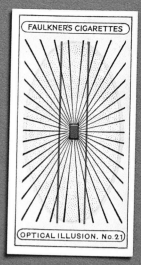

FAULKNER'S CIGARETTES

OPTICAL ILLUSION. No. 21.

DAVIES'S CIGARETTES.

Outside guard with left.

CLARKE'S CIGARETTES.

ROYAL MAIL MOTOR VAN.

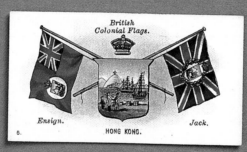

British Colonial Flags.

Ensign.   Jack.

HONG KONG.

MITCHELL'S CIGARETTES.

BANBURY CROSS.

LAMBERT & BUTLER'S CIGARETTES.   FN

CANTERBURY. MONKS INFIRMARY.

LAMBERT & BUTLER'S CIGARETTES.   NH

NORTHAMPTON. THE GUILDHALL.

BRIXHAM.

HARLECH CASTLE.

CHAPTER 5

THE IMPERIAL BRANCHES

In the previous chapter we reviewed the card issues of Wills, John Player and Ogden's, who were the main branches of the Imperial Tobacco Company following the settlement of the Tobacco War in 1902. We can now take a brief look at the background and card issues of the other members of the ITC. After the purchase of Ogden's from American Tobacco the structure of the group changed little until some time after World War I. The business of J & F Bell Limited of Glasgow was, however, acquired in 1904 and merged with the Stephen Mitchell branch. For convenience, their issues are included in this chapter.

Apart from the small London based Hignett's Tobacco Co Limited, all the other branches issued cards both before and after the formation of the ITC. Increasingly after 1902 it will be found that the same basic set would be issued by one or more of the branches and these are generally only distinguishable by the name of the sponsoring firm. This is a problem common to

other groups outside the ITC and, indeed, existed in the very early days when sets of actresses or soldiers would be issued by several different manufacturers. Most of the ITC cards were printed and designed by Mardon, Son & Hall, who built up an enviable reputation for quality, accuracy and style.

ADKIN & SONS

The person who gave the firm its name was Mrs Margaret Adkin. She took over the snuff-making business founded by her father in 1775 and gave it new direction and impetus. The early card issues concentrated on actresses, beauties and soldiers, some of which were premium cards exchangeable for 'Cabinet Proofs'. The set of 12 A ROYAL FAVOURITE could possibly have been issued for Queen Victoria's Diamond Jubilee and, unusually, featured only the female members of the British and European royal families.

After the formation of the ITC, card issues were suspended and did not recommence until 1914 when a scarce set of 30 SPORTING CUPS & TROPHIES was distributed. Two more series in black and white completed Adkin's wartime quota and then between 1922 and 1924 they put out nicely printed re-issues of two 20 year old Player sets – BUTTERFLIES & MOTHS and WILD ANIMALS OF THE WORLD. At one time the Adkin printings were a cheap way to acquire these well designed sets, but no longer. As is the case with many issues of the smaller companies between the wars, limited print runs have ensured a marked escalation in prices. Sadly, these reprints concluded the firm's output and in 1946 they were merged into the W & F Faulkner branch.

Adkin **A Royal Favourite**, c1900 (J, set of 12)

Adkin **Sporting Cups & Trophies**, 1914 (D, per card)

page 60

Left to right

Top row, first and second cards:
Adkin **Butterflies & Moths**, 1924 (H, set of 50)

Top row, third and fourth cards:
Faulkner **Optical Illusions**, 1935 (G, set of 25)

Middle row:
Davies **Boxing**, 1924 (H, set of 25)
Clarke **Royal Mail**, 1914 (C, per card) (top card)
Edwards, Ringer & Bigg **Flags of All Nations***
(stag back), 1907 (C, per card) (bottom card)
Mitchell **Famous Crosses**, 1923 (D, set of 25)

Bottom row, first and second cards:
Lambert & Butler **Motor Index Marks**, 1926 (I, set of 50)

Bottom row, third and fourth cards:
Smith **Holiday Resorts**, 1925 (J, set of 25)

W A & A C CHURCHMAN

This famous firm from Ipswich in Suffolk is another with its roots in the 18th century. It remained a minor family business until the mid-1880s when a combination of the growth in demand for cigarettes and the management of the firm by the two young brothers, William and Arthur, coincided. A new factory was constructed in Portman Road, also the home of the equally well-known football club. In 1898 and 1899 two famous brands were launched – Top Score and Tenner. The former originally had the cricketer Ranjitsinhji pictured on the front of the packet and the latter was the colloquial name for a £10.00 note, which in those days must have been a rare sight. Interestingly, advertisements of this era stated that packs contained 'photos' rather than cards, this being the terminology used by others, including Ogden's with their Guinea Gold brand.

These early cards were the usual series of actresses and beauties issued also by many other firms and the advent of the Boer War brought with it issues known as TYPES OF BRITISH AND COLONIAL TROOPS*, BOER WAR GENERALS* and HOME AND COLONIAL REGIMENTS*. When the Tobacco War started Churchman's stayed on the sidelines until eventually joining on the Imperial side in May 1902. Cards continued to appear at regular intervals through to 1914 but the management were content to follow the pattern set by other members of the group. EAST SUFFOLK CHURCHES, first issued in 1912, was the only concession to local interest and this black and white series was reissued in 1917 and 1923.

A change of policy saw some original series appearing in Churchman's brands. An attractive set of action pictures of FOOTBALLERS was issued

in November 1914 and then the following year they distributed 50 SILHOUETTES OF WARSHIPS taken from *Jane's Fighting Ships*. WEST SUFFOLK CHURCHES was notable for being one of very few series to be produced between 1917 and 1922. RIVERS & BROADS OF NORFOLK & SUFFOLK continued the local theme until the end of 1922 when a new and distinctive style emerged.

Over the next ten years around 20 different standard sized series of 25 cards were produced, mainly in colour, on a wonderful variety of subjects. The compilers really excelled themselves in inventiveness, with CURIOUS DWELLINGS, THE INNS OF COURT, INTERESTING DOOR-KNOCKERS, FAMOUS CRICKET COLOURS, MUSICAL INSTRUMENTS, PIPES OF THE WORLD, NATURE'S ARCHITECTS and INTERESTING EXPERIMENTS, being just a few of the titles. Some of these standard sized cards also appeared as sets of 12 in large sized cards, which was a policy continued when the sets of 25 were phased out in favour of the more normal complement of 50.

Trains were a popular and recurring subject from RAILWAY WORKING in 1926 through to the 1937 series of WONDERFUL RAILWAY TRAVEL. The sea was another favourite topic with LIFE IN A LINER, THE STORY OF NAVIGATION and, perhaps, best of the lot THE 'QUEEN MARY'. In this latter series we can see the original design models, the launch by the Queen in 1934 (using a bottle of Australian wine) and the extensive fitting out work. The tobacconist's shop is, of course,

Churchman **Footballers** (coloured), 1914 (C, per card)

page 63
Churchman, *top to bottom*

Left row:
Curious Dwellings, 1926 (G, set of 25)
Prominent Golfers, 1931 (C, per card)
Nature's Architects, 1930 (F, set of 25)

Middle row:
Silhouettes of Warships, 1915 (C, per card)
Rivers & Broads of Norfolk & Suffolk, 1922 (B, per card)
Interesting Door-Knockers, 1928 (G, set of 25)
Pipes of the World, 1927 (G, set of 25)
Interesting Experiments, 1929 (F, set of 25)

Right row:
Curious Signs, 1925 (G, set of 25)
The Inns of Court, 1922 (G, set of 25)
Lawn Tennis, 1928 (I, set of 50)

CHURCHMAN'S CIGARETTES.

A CHIEF'S HUT, FIJI.

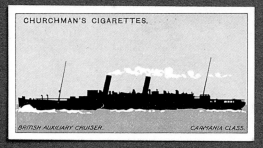

CHURCHMAN'S CIGARETTES.

BRITISH AUXILIARY CRUISER. CARMANIA CLASS.

CHURCHMAN'S CIGARETTES.

THE "NOW THUS".

CHURCHMAN'S CIGARETTES.

THE YARE, BRUNDALL.

CHURCHMAN'S CIGARETTES

R. MACKENZIE

CHURCHMAN'S CIGARETTES

13TH CENTURY KNOCKER.

NEW HALL, LINCOLN'S INN, EXTERIOR

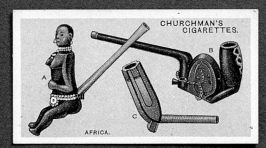

CHURCHMAN'S CIGARETTES

AFRICA.

CHURCHMAN'S CIGARETTES.

THE HARVEST MOUSE.

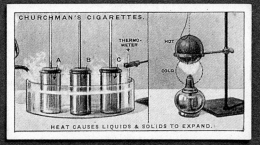

CHURCHMAN'S CIGARETTES.

THERMO-METER HOT

COLD

A B C

HEAT CAUSES LIQUIDS & SOLIDS TO EXPAND.

CHURCHMAN'S CIGARETTES

MISS BETTY NUTHALL.
(GREAT BRITAIN).

Churchman
Left to right
The RAF at Work, 1938
(G, set of 48 medium)

Churchman **Kings of Speed**,
1939 (F, set of 50)

Clarke **Sporting Terms***,
c1900 (G, per card)

featured and card no.44 showing girls of the Queen Mary School, Lytham, at work on the Blue Ensign, is alone worth the price of the set.

Two excellent sporting caricature sets were produced, MEN OF THE MOMENT IN SPORT from 1929 and the 1931 series of SPORTING CELEBRITIES. Even more prized by collectors are the sets of PROMINENT GOLFERS and FAMOUS GOLFERS. This latter issue from 1927 was printed in sepia as was the 1928 series of LAWN TENNIS. A similar style was used in the late 1930s for BOXING PERSONALITIES, two series of 50 ASSOCIATION FOOTBALLERS and KINGS OF SPEED. In this latter set we can find the champion sprinter Jesse Owens, the £100 per week speedway ace, 'Bluey' Wilkinson and world water speed record holder, Sir Malcolm Campbell.

In 1937 Churchman started to distribute some distinctive medium sized cards in sets of 48. These are not expensive and are well worth collecting. Most sought after is THE RAF AT WORK but equally attractive is WINGS OVER THE EMPIRE. The series produced by many of the ITC branches, AIR-RAID PRECAUTIONS, was printed in this medium format and is most effective. After the 1939/45 war Churchman retained its relative independence for some years and by 1965 had absorbed the Lambert & Butler and Edwards, Ringer & Bigg branches. A later reorganisation saw the phasing out of cigarette production and then in 1973 cigar manufacture was moved to John Player and the tobacco side was taken over by Ogden's.

WM CLARKE & SON

The firm was founded in Cork about 1830 but later moved its manufacturing base to Liverpool. Card issues were not extensive, possibly because the firm concentrated on hand-made cigarettes sold by weight. The attractively shaped TOBACCO LEAF GIRLS* series is among the very scarcest of cigarette card issues. A humorous series of SPORTING TERMS* appeared around 1900 and the next year a CRICKETER SERIES of black and white cards was produced.

A similar style set of 66 footballers was distributed at about the time of the Tobacco War.

Having come under the umbrella of the ITC the branch concentrated on sales of tobacco and no new cards were issued until 1907, when an attractive MARINE SERIES appeared. Thereafter just three more issues were distributed, all duplicating series from other ITC branches. After the formation of the Irish Free State the business relocated back to Ireland with Ogden's taking over responsibility for the UK brands.

Williams **Views of Chester**, c1912 (E, per card)

W T DAVIES & SONS
W WILLIAMS & CO

It is convenient to look at these two Chester-based firms together as their businesses were closely linked for many years. Both organisations were founded in the first half of the 19th century and both joined the ITC on 1 May 1902 at the height of the Tobacco War.

Early card issues were few – a short set of ACTRESSES* from Davies and 25 BOER WAR CELEBRITIES* from Williams. Davies also put out two titled series, NEWPORT FOOTBALL CLUB and ROYAL WELSH FUSILIERS, that are very rarely seen today. In 1912 Williams produced a series of 12 VIEWS OF CHESTER and followed up a year later with a second. Little original material was produced after this and in 1954 the businesses were merged into the Faulkner branch.

EDWARDS, RINGER & BIGG

Founded in 1813 the firm, usually referred to as 'ERB', was the smallest of the three Bristol companies that were founder members of the ITC. The business of W O Bigg & Co had been acquired in 1893 but some dozen years later they issued two series under their old name. Otherwise the cards refer to Ringer's Cigarettes or give the full name of the firm. Among the very earliest issues is a series of three cards, EASTER MANOEUVRES OF OUR VOLUNTEERS, which is extremely rare. The sets of 25 BEAUTIES* and BOER WAR CELEBRITIES* put out around the turn of the century had calendar backs for 1900 and 1901 respectively thus enabling accurate dating.

In 1905 LIFE ON BOARD A MAN OF WAR was issued both by ERB and W O Bigg and this was followed in 1906 by BIRDS AND EGGS*. The DOGS SERIES*, being 23 cards from the composite series of FOWLS PIGEONS AND DOGS, can be collected with Klondyke Cigarettes or Exmoor Hunt Mixture backs, the latter being the scarcer. FLAGS OF ALL NATIONS is even more complex as the 37 cards can be collected with and without the series title, numbered and unnumbered and with various different prices quoted for Exmoor Hunt Mixture. During 1911 and 1912 three series of 25 photogravure cards were distributed of ABBEYS AND CASTLES, ALPINE

VIEWS and COAST AND COUNTRY. Again there are back variations to look for.

During the First World War two series of sectional maps were issued showing the Western Front. The first was in colour and consisted of 56 cards and the second with 54 cards was printed in monochrome. When card issues resumed after the war most of the series distributed by ERB, such as CELEBRATED BRIDGES, MINING, OPTICAL ILLUSIONS and GARDEN LIFE, had previously been used by the larger branches. CINEMA STARS dating from 1923, which can be collected either as 50 standard size or 25 large cards, was a novel issue for the time and HOW TO TELL FORTUNES remains one of the few sets in the catalogue on this subject. The cards illustrate the various star signs then go on to show how to tell fortunes by using both playing cards and tea leaves. Finally, the mysteries of palmistry are explained.

In the 1940s and 1950s ERB expanded by acquiring the businesses of some of the other branches until, as part of the 1965 restructuring, it was merged with the Churchman branch.

W & F FAULKNER

This London based firm was established in 1838 and became a limited company in 1896. Prior to joining the ITC in 1902 they were fairly prolific issuers of many different series of cards but in such small numbers that none of them are easy to find today. As might be expected, actresses and beauties were among the early issues but a feature of the firm's output was the large number of series that consisted of 12 cards. These all had plain backs and many of them were of a humorous nature. The PUZZLE SERIES* is probably the earliest dating from about 1898 and the others followed over the next two or three years. Of special note are the illustrations of various 'terms' such as CRICKET TERMS, FOOTBALL TERMS, POLICE TERMS* and so on.

Some patriotic series were distributed during the Boer War, including SOUTH AFRICAN WAR SCENES*, and 40 cards were issued of KINGS AND QUEENS* to mark the Coronation of King Edward VII. The last distribution before joining

W O Bigg **Life on Board a Man of War**, c1905
(C, per card)

Faulkner **Kings and Queens***, 1902 (E, per card)

65

FORTUNE-TELLING. ASTROLOGY.

LIBRA—THE BALANCE
THE SIGN FOR OCTOBER.

SCORPIO—THE SCORPION
THE SIGN FOR NOVEMBER.

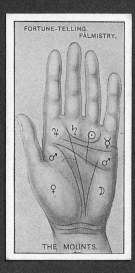

FORTUNE-TELLING.
PALMISTRY.

THE MOUNTS.

FAWN PUG.

RINGER'S
CIGARETTES

BULL-DOG.

RINGER'S
CIGARETTES

RINGER'S CIGARETTES.

BRIDGE OVER THE MOSELLE.

HIGNETT'S CIGARETTES.

WINSTON CHURCHILL.

RINGER'S CIGARETTES.

BRIDGE OF THE RIALTO, VENICE.

Hignett's Cigarettes.

The Capitol, Washington.

Hignett's Cigarettes.

Place Dom Pedro, Lisbon.

HIGNETT'S
CIGARETTES.

SWITZERLAND.
BON JOUR. COMMENT
ALLEZ-VOUS?"

HIGNETT'S
CIGARETTES.

MEXICO.
"BUENOS DIAS. ¿CÓMO SIGUE?"

HIGNETT'S
CIGARETTES.

ITALY.
"BUON GIORNO. COME VA TU?"

HIGNETT'S
CIGARETTES.

ABYSSINIA.
"ENDIET ALLOO?"

the ITC was OUR GALLANT GRENADIERS where the first 20 of the 40 card series can be collected both with and without the ITC Clause.

After 1902 card issues inexplicably ceased and it was not until 1923 that Faulkner brands once again contained cards. PROMINENT RACEHORSES OF THE PRESENT DAY appeared in two series of 25 but the sets that followed can all be found issued by one or more of the other branches. OUR PETS, issued also by Edwards, Ringer & Bigg in 1926, is very attractive and a must for anyone interested in domestic animals. Having taken over the Adkin's branch in 1946, Faulkner was itself absorbed by Ogden's in 1959.

FRANKLYN, DAVEY & CO

The business was started around 1780 by George Franklyn at Welsh Back, Bristol and in 1827 his two sons took over the management. Thomas Davey became a partner in 1859 and it was his descendants who became directors of the ITC in 1901. The firm's first cards had appeared earlier, in about 1896, and consisted of an untitled series of 50 birds in colour. A short series of 10 cards of TYPES OF SMOKERS followed and in 1901 they issued, in common with other manufacturers, BOER WAR GENERALS* and STAR GIRLS*. These latter items are very scarce.

After joining the ITC cards appeared at irregular intervals, both before and after World War I, but all mirrored series issued elsewhere in the group until 1925. In that year they put

out a series of 25 sepia cards of HUNTING exclusively devoted to fox hunting. Not a subject that finds universal favour today but then very much a part of country life.

Five years on and another unusual series was produced of MODERN DANCE STEPS. The first 50 cards were followed by a second series in 1931. The illustrations show the then prominent instructor and band leader, Victor Silvestor, demonstrating how to get round the floor in, for example, the Quickstep and the Blues. Not the most colourful series ever issued but certainly different and very topical at the time. In 1957 the Franklyn, Davey branch was merged into its near neighbour, Edwards, Ringer & Bigg.

Left:
Franklyn, Davey **Modern Dance Steps** (1st Series), 1929 (B, per card)

Right:
Franklyn, Davey **Hunting**, 1925 (E, set of 25)

HIGNETT BROS & CO

It was not surprising that Hignett opted to join the ITC in 1901 after their Liverpool neighbours and rivals, Ogden's Limited, had been bought out by James Duke. Early card issues were quite enterprising with 60 ANIMAL PICTURES and a series of 20 YACHTS* being produced before the turn of the century. THE CABINET, 1900 featured the Marquis of Salisbury, Mr A J Balfour and various other politicians of the day. A series of 25 actresses in photogravure was issued with their Golden Butterfly cigarettes and another leading brand, Pilot, packed a further 28 actresses including Anna Held, wife of the Broadway impresario, Florenz Ziegfeld.

INTERESTING BUILDINGS, issued in 1905, is a lovely lithographed set picturing the Colosseum in Rome, the Kremlin and even the Chief's House, Tupuselei, New Guinea. Another charming set is GREETINGS OF THE WORLD which although originally issued in 1907, was distributed again in 1923, and consequently is

---

page 66, left to right
Edwards, Ringer & Bigg

Top row, first and second cards:
How to tell Fortunes, 1929 (I, set of 25)

Third and fourth cards:
Dogs* (Klondyke back), 1908 (H, set of 23)

Second row, first and last cards:
Celebrated Bridges, 1924 (I, set of 50)

Middle card: Hignett **Modern Statesmen**, 1906 (J, set of 25)

Third row:
Hignett **Interesting Buildings**, 1905 (B, per card)

Fourth row:
Hignett **Greetings of the World**, 1907 (H, set of 25)

Hignett **Actresses 'PILPI I'***, c1901 (D, per card)

Hignett **Cathedrals & Churches**, 1909 (I, set of 25)

not quite so expensive as some other issues of this period. MODERN STATESMEN, whilst not so colourful, is full of interest. On card no.5 is pictured the MP for Oldham, a young Winston Churchill.

The first new issue after World War I, released in January 1924, was COMMON OBJECTS OF THE SEA-SHORE and later that year another series of 25 cards pictured THE PRINCE OF WALES' EMPIRE TOUR*. INTERNATIONAL CAPS AND BADGES and SHIPS FLAGS & CAP BADGES were attractive coloured series following a similar format. The latter was sufficiently popular to generate a second series which was distributed in July 1927. Hignett also issued some series in monochrome which were, nevertheless, very interesting, including CELEBRATED OLD INNS, HISTORICAL LONDON and TURNPIKES. The latter includes an interesting picture of Tottenham Court Road as it appeared in 1812.

In 1930 the Hignett branch was merged into Ogden's and, although cards continued to be produced to a very high standard, the designs were all similar to those of the parent organisation. SEA ADVENTURE in 1939 closed the chapter on what had been an impressive record of stimulating card issues.

Lambert & Butler **Advertisement Card***, c1898 (K, per card)

LAMBERT & BUTLER

Two school chums, Charles Lambert and Charles Butler, started the firm in 1834 with premises in Clerkenwell. The business soon moved to Drury Lane and not long after, in 1842, Charles Butler married Sarah Lambert, the youngest sister of his partner. They were one of the leading cigar houses and prominent manufacturers of cigarettes. May Blossom and the more successful Waverley were among the brands marketed towards the end of the 19th century. The firm was changed to a limited company in 1898 and when the Tobacco War started Charles Edward Lambert and Walter Butler, sons of the founders, were running the business and became directors of the ITC.

The first card issued by the firm was a handsome advertisement card known as the 'Spanish Dancer' and the first series was probably a set of 10 ACTRESSES AND THEIR AUTOGRAPHS*. A very interesting set of the early period depicted 10 prominent JOCKEYS*. The back of these cards listed many of the brands available and stated whether they could be purchased in packets, boxes, tins or by weight.

The JAPANESE SERIES from 1904 was another issue where the back was as interesting as the front but this time because of the intricate Japanese screen design. The delightful WAVERLEY SERIES* was also produced in 1904 and featured characters from Sir Walter Scott's novels. A beautifully printed set, one of the best of its type, is the series of 40 ARMS OF KINGS & QUEENS OF ENGLAND. Some of the cards depict the arms against a black background which is most effective. In 1908 the classic set of 25 MOTORS was produced, the first of many on this theme. The WORLD'S LOCOMOTIVES was the title for three separate series during the years 1912 to 1914 and two other sets with a difference that must be mentioned are WIRELESS TELEGRAPHY and WINTER SPORTS.

In 1922 the motor car theme was continued with four excellent series appearing during the inter-war years. Several related series were produced including MOTOR CAR RADIATORS, HINTS & TIPS FOR MOTORISTS, HOW MOTOR CARS WORK and MOTOR CYCLES. Aviation was another favourite theme with A HISTORY OF AVIATION put out in 1932, repeated with brown fronts a year later, FAMOUS BRITISH AIRMEN & AIRWOMEN, EMPIRE AIR ROUTES and, from 1937, AEROPLANE MARKINGS. In between times a superb set of DANCE BAND LEADERS was issued featuring many of the famous names that were heard on the wireless each weekday evening.

The branch largely avoided the trend towards adhesive cards but one set certainly worth collecting is LONDON CHARACTERS. The 25 cards can be found with and without an album clause, although the latter are quite scarce. The set was issued in 1934, the year of the firm's centenary, when the celebrations included a dinner for the staff of 750. The last set issued in October 1939 was as good as anything produced previously and the title tells all – INTERESTING SIDELIGHTS ON THE WORK OF THE GPO. After the Second World War the branch finally lost its independence when, in 1965, Churchman took over responsibility for all the brands.

D & J MACDONALD

This Glasgow firm was founded in 1840 by Duncan and Jones MacDonald, and at the time of the formation of the ITC it was resident at 60 Glassford Street. Around the turn of the century a short series of ACTRESSES* was distributed and, surprisingly for a Scottish firm, a series of 25 CRICKETERS*. All the cards issued by the firm are exceedingly rare. No series were produced after 1902 and in 1918 the business was transferred to the F & J Smith branch.

Lambert & Butler
Dance Band Leaders, 1936
(I, set of 25)

STEPHEN MITCHELL & SON

This firm started as far back as 1723 in Linlithgow as grocers but tobacco products became a regular line and manufacturing commenced in 1741. By 1825 the business had relocated to Glasgow where the firm was based when they became founder members of the ITC. The earliest card issues were of ACTORS AND ACTRESSES* which advertised their best-selling Prize Crop brand. A series of black and white BOXER REBELLION – SKETCHES* was distributed in 1901 and about the same date a lovely set of REGIMENTAL CRESTS, NICKNAMES AND COLLAR BADGES* made its appearance.

After settlement of the Tobacco War the ITC acquired J & F Bell Ltd, also based in Glasgow, and merged the business into that of Stephen Mitchell. Both firms issued a colourful production, SCOTTISH CLAN SERIES, with the Bell's cards being packed with their aptly named Three Bells brand of cigarettes. Mitchell, in common with other branches, distributed the set of 50 INTERESTING BUILDINGS but the series of 25 SPORTS was unique to the firm. With superbly lithographed fronts and a delightful *art nouveau* design on the back, this is one of the most attractive series of the period.

Mitchell

Top to bottom, left row:
Arms & Armour, 1916
(K, set of 50)

Middle row:
Famous Scots, 1933
(F, set of 50)

Right row:
Interesting Buildings, 1905
(B, per card)

Mitchell **Clan Tartans**
(1st Series), 1927
(H, set of 50)

After the start of the First World War Mitchell issued the old Player ARMS & ARMOUR set and also 25 MEDALS* based on the series put out by F & J Smith but with white backgrounds. Two series of BRITISH WARSHIPS were produced in 1915, including a card illustrating HMS Amphion, which we are told was the first British ship lost during the war. During the inter-war period the branch not only put out a number of series with a Scottish flavour, it also broke new ground with FAMOUS CROSSES, HUMOROUS DRAWINGS, RIVER & COASTAL STEAMERS and LONDON CEREMONIALS. During the 1930s its two 'gallery' series for 1934 and 1935, THE WORLD OF TOMORROW and WONDERFUL CENTURY were all highly acclaimed, despite being printed in a single brownish tone.

Of Scottish interest were two series of CLAN TARTANS, a set of 50 covering SCOTLAND'S STORY and another 50 featuring FAMOUS SCOTS. These were all in colour and in addition there were two series in sepia of SCOTTISH FOOTBALLERS and SCOTTISH FOOTBALL SNAPS. The set of FAMOUS SCOTS pictures a different personality on each card within an oval frame with an adjacent line drawing depicting an important event in their life. The series commences with Macbeth, shows the reformist John Knox on card no.9 and on card no.27 the brave and charming Flora

MacDonald. The painter, Sir Henry Raeburn, the inventor James Watt and former Prime Minister, the Earl of Balfour, all find a place in this fascinating series.

In 1933 the F & J Smith branch was absorbed but in 1957 Mitchell were themselves merged into W D & H O Wills.

RICHMOND CAVENDISH CO LTD

The two Liverpool firms of Cope Bros and Hignett Bros were instrumental in the founding of Richmond Cavendish, which was incorporated in 1865. The business grew out of the need to obtain sweetened tobacco when the American Civil War cut off supplies. Mr John Hignett played a leading role in the management of the company and guided it into the ITC as a founder member in 1901.

A number of early series of actresses and beauties were issued, some in common with Hignett and other firms. A long series of ACTRESSES* printed in photogravure was issued with Pioneer cigarettes, and type cards can still be obtained fairly readily. Not so common but more attractive is the set of 52 BEAUTIES* with playing card inset. Other sets issued together with Hignett's, such as MUSIC HALL ARTISTES* and YACHTS*, are not often seen.

Control of Richmond Cavendish was passed to

Richmond Cavendish
Beauties* (P/C Inset), c1897
(G, per card)

71

page 73

Smith **Advertisement Cards***, c1897 (K, per card)

Smith **Phil May Sketches*** (brown back), 1924 (B, per card)

Smith **Fowls Pigeons & Dogs**, 1908 (C, per card)

BAT when that company was formed in 1902 and the Hignett branch acquired the UK brand names. The 1920's sets of CHINESE ACTORS AND ACTRESSES* and CINEMA STARS were issued under the auspices of BAT.

F & J SMITH

The great expansion of trade which took place in Glasgow after the union in 1707 included a substantial percentage of the tobacco imports entering the British Isles. It is not surprising that F & J Smith grew up alongside D & J MacDonald and Stephen Mitchell as important and prosperous manufacturers of tobacco products. As we have seen it lost its independence to Mitchell during the inter-war period but left a rich legacy of attractive and interesting cards. Not least among them are the early advertisement cards of which 24 basic types have been recorded. Smith not only had a wide range of brands, they tended to print a mixture of these brands on the backs of their cards. For those who seek completeness, this poses an almost insoluble task where there can be up to 15 different backs to each picture.

The firm was among the first to issue a series of FOOTBALLERS, no less than 120 being featured with their Cup Tie cigarettes. The series known as CHAMPIONS OF SPORT* included a number of cricketers including Dr W G Grace and the Indian born genius, K S Ranjitsinhji. A TOUR ROUND THE WORLD is a favourite set of many, the version with the postcard back being the most interesting but also the most expensive. FOWLS PIGEONS & DOGS, much copied by other branches, is attractively presented and for a good chuckle the PHIL MAY SKETCHES* are worth collecting. These were also reprinted after the war with different backs.

FAMOUS EXPLORERS from 1911 and BATTLEFIELDS OF GREAT BRITAIN issued in 1913 are a little different, both in design and subject matter, to most other contemporary series. The set of 50 FOOTBALL CLUB RECORDS is also unusual, and confusing, in that the results of the clubs printed on the reverse cover seasons ranging from 1913-14 to 1916-17. Making shadowgraphs was a popular children's pastime 80 years ago and Smith produced a series of 25 examples in April 1915. After the 1914/18 war just six further series were issued. PROMINENT RUGBY PLAYERS consisted of nice action sketches by the artist H F Crowther-Smith and HOLIDAY RESORTS in July 1925 featured attractive railway posters of, among other places, Brixham, Clacton and Lowestoft.

F. & J. SMITH'S

Shooting Lodge Cigarettes.

F. & J. Smith's

Harvest Moon
Tobacco & Cigarettes.

F. & J. SMITH'S

Cut Golden Bar.

GLASGOW

F. & J. SMITH'S

Sun Cured
Mixture.

GLASGOW

MANUFACTURED BY

F & J. SMITH.
GLASGOW

Pen & Pencil
CIGARETTES

Pen & Pencil

F. & J. SMITH'S

BRIGHT
FLAKE TOBACCO.

MANUFACTURED BY

SMITH'S
Wild Geranium
CIGARETTES

F & J. SMITH.
GLASGOW

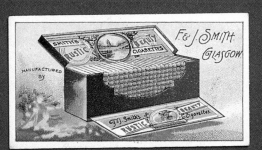

SMITH'S
RUSTIC
BEAUTY
CIGARETTES

F. & J. SMITH.
GLASGOW

MANUFACTURED BY

F & J. Smith's
RUSTIC Cigarettes

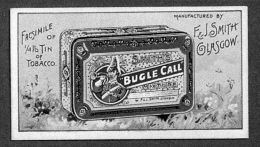

FACSIMILE
OF
¼ lb TIN
OF
TOBACCO.

MANUFACTURED BY

F. & J. SMITH.
GLASGOW.

SMITH'S
"BUGLE CALL"
MIXTURE

F. & J. SMITH'S

ALBION FLAKE TOBACCO.

F. & J. SMITH'S

Glasgow Mixture
TOBACCO

F. & J. Smith's

GOLDEN BAR
TOBACCO.

F. & J. SMITH'S

Glasgow
Mixture

TOBACCO.
GLASGOW.

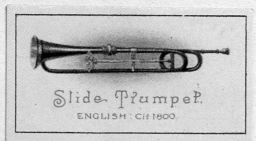

Slide Trumpet.
ENGLISH : Cir 1800

GRETA GARBO

HAPPY FANNY FIELDS

I'VE JUST COME FROM GERMANY.

THE PROOF OF THE PUDDING IS IN THE EATING

LICHFIELD

OSTRICH

YACHT RACING.
SPORTS & PASTIMES. SERIES I. Nº5.

Elsie and Doris Waters

DIANA CHURCHILL

CHAPTER 6

THE INDEPENDENTS

When the dust had settled after the Tobacco War there were still several hundred independent companies fighting for market share against the might of the ITC. But as the years went by the rationalisation process continued and by 1940 many firms had closed or merged with others, leaving a smaller number of larger groups. The reasons were many but the cost of mechanisation, the spread of branded products through advertising, the bulk buying power of the major companies and the lower unit costs resulting from longer production runs, were all contributory factors.

In a book of this size it is not possible to review all the firms that issued cards. The larger groups and companies with meaningful card issuing policies are listed separately. However, a few of the smaller companies are covered at the end of this chapter. On the whole those firms that were absorbed by others during the 1902-1940 period are mentioned together with their parent organisation.

page 74, top to bottom

Left row:
Ardath **Proverbs**, 1936 (D, set of 25)
Cope **Cathedrals**, 1939 (F, set of 25)
Phillips **Red Indians**, 1927 (G, set of 25)

Middle row:
CWS **Musical Instruments**, 1934
(J, set of 48)
Hill **Historic Places from Dickens' Classics**, 1926
(F, set of 50 large)
Morris **Whipsnade Zoo**, 1932 (D, set of 50)
Taddy **Sports & Pastimes**, 1912 (D, per card)
John Sinclair **Radio Favourites**, 1935 (H, set of 54)

Right row:
Carreras **Film Favourites**, 1938 (G, set of 50)
Cohen Weenen **Star Artistes**, c1907 (C, per card)
Gallaher **My Favourite Part**, 1939 (F, set of 48)

ARDATH TOBACCO CO LTD

Founded in 1896 by Sir Albert Levy, the business originally manufactured exclusive and quality lines for the fashionable smokers of the day. No cards were issued until just before the outbreak of the 1914/18 war, by which time the firm had expanded sufficiently to have set up a factory and branch in Holland. The first cards were photogravure reproductions of paintings by famous masters, mostly of medium size, in sets of 30. Some of them, such as the REMBRANDT SERIES and RUBENS SERIES, were distributed in Holland and some were inserted in export packs for New Zealand and elsewhere. Smokers could obtain specially illustrated books by collecting the series and sending in the cards to the address printed on the back.

Ardath had not resumed card issues when in 1925 the business was acquired jointly by BAT and the ITC. Although a few series of cards were inserted by BAT in export packs they were not immediately used in the UK. After the end of the coupon era in 1934 cards at last became a major marketing tool. No doubt the policy change also dictated that the cards should be 'different' and over the following six years the style of Ardath's issues was so distinctive there was no danger that they could be mistaken for those of any other manufacturer.

Basically, the standard sized card series had varnished fronts and adhesive backs and special albums were produced. FAMOUS FILM STARS from August 1934 was a little different in that it was non-adhesive and carried no descriptive text. The set of 50 FAMOUS FOOTBALLERS which followed in October was complete with text and in this series we can find a youthful Stanley Matthews and two Arsenal stalwarts, Eddie

Ardath **Famous Film Stars**, 1934 (G, set of 50)

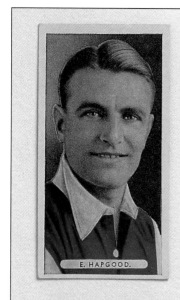

E. HAPGOOD.

SUPERMARINE S-6B.

KATHARINE HEPBURN

WIGAN R.L.F.C.

HELEN JACOBS

WHO IS THE WORLD'S SWEETHEART?

H.R.H. THE DUCHESS OF YORK
At the time of Her Wedding

Ardath, *top to bottom*

Left row:
Famous Footballers, 1934 (G, set of 50). **Cricket, Tennis & Golf Celebrities**, 1935 (G, set of 50)

Middle row:
Speed – Land, Sea & Air, 1935 (G, set of 50)
Photocards 'A' (Lancashire Football Teams), 1936 (I, set of 110 large)
Who is This?, 1936 (H, set of 50)

Right row:
Film, Stage and Radio Stars, 1935 (G, set of 50)
Silver Jubilee, 1935 (F, set of 50)

Hapgood and Alex James. A very interesting set of 50 from 1935 was SPEED–LAND, SEA & AIR. This pictured the outright Schneider Trophy winner, the Supermarine S-6B, and from Germany an early diesel train unit, the 'Flying Hamburger'. For one of their last standard sized sets issued in 1939 Ardath changed the format, discarded the varnish and the adhesive, and produced STAMPS RARE & INTERESTING. This was deservedly voted 'Set of the Year' by the members of the Cartophilic Society.

Before that, in 1936, Ardath had started to issue photographic cards, called PHOTOCARDS, of which Series A consisted of 110 Lancashire football teams. Within a couple of months Series B through F, all of regional football teams, were appearing in cigarette packets and collectors must have been tearing their hair out trying to obtain all 715 cards issued. But the concept did enable some very junior clubs to find cartophilic glory, such as Greenbank Methodists and Kenilworth Early Closers. In 1937 the subject matter was widened to include film stars and other celebrities and the cards were stated to be 'A Continuous Series of Topical Interest'. In addition to the PHOTOCARDS several series titled REAL PHOTOGRAPHS were produced, so collectors specialising in these cards are sure of a testing time.

After cigarette cards had been discontinued, Ardath, under the auspices of the Ministry of Information, distributed what can only be described as propaganda items. IT ALL DEPENDS ON ME consisted of 24 cards praising the war efforts of many workers on the home front. Various information slips were also issued, plus 48 paper inserts on HOW TO RECOGNISE THE SERVICE RANKS.

CARRERAS LTD

It was Jose Josquin Carreras, a young Spanish entrepreneur, who gave his name to this business when he acquired an old established tobacconist shop in London in 1846. His speciality was blending mixtures of tobacco for wealthy and discriminating clients, who included the then Prince of Wales. Craven Mixture, for many years a best seller, was named after the Third Earl of Craven. The business was made into a limited company in 1903, by which time it had come under the control of Bernhard Baron. This charismatic American had emigrated from Russia as a youngster and was the inventor of the Baron Cigarette Making Machine.

The machine enabled the firm to break into the mass produced cigarette market with the popular Black Cat brand. The cat from which the name was derived was apparently famous for making his home in the Carreras shop window during the 1880s. Although various promotional

schemes were used, including coupons and postage stamps, cards did not feature until 1916.

The first card series to appear was the dramatic and controversial RAEMAEKERS WAR CARTOONS. This long series of cards can be collected with either Black Cat or Carreras Cigarettes printed on the front. These vitriolic sketches on the barbarity of the enemy so infuriated the Germans that they put a price on the Belgian artist's head. WOMEN ON WAR WORK was a refreshingly different series and the 50 cards show nicely printed vignettes of women carrying out essential tasks formerly the prerogative of the male.

The SCIENCE OF BOXING was an early and colourful issue soon after the war had ended and these cards also had separate printings for Black Cat and Carreras Cigarettes. FIGURES OF FICTION and HIGHWAYMEN both appeared in 1924 each as a series of 25. J M Barrie was one of Carreras' notable customers, so it is not surprising that Peter Pan featured in the former set. Alexander Boguslavsky Ltd, famous for their Turf and Piccadilly cigarettes, had been acquired in 1913. They issued five different series between 1923 and 1925, of which SPORTS RECORDS* and WINNERS ON THE TURF are the easiest to acquire. From 1925 four sets were issued by Carreras in standard, large and extra large sizes with the legend Turf Cigarettes on the reverse. RACES – HISTORIC & MODERN is probably the pick of these sets and featured a number of competitive sports.

For a period of about ten years from the late 1920s Carreras put out a number of varied and interesting series but towards the end of the 1930s they rather over-issued real photos of glamour girls and film stars. Nevertheless BRITISH COSTUMES, CELEBRITIES OF BRITISH HISTORY, FLOWERS, FAMOUS AIRMEN & AIRWOMEN, TOOLS AND HOW TO USE THEM and BIRDS OF THE COUNTRYSIDE are just a few of the sets that are worth a place in any collection. Two sets from 1937, HISTORY OF ARMY UNIFORMS and HISTORY OF NAVAL UNIFORMS, are both informative and attractive. The series of 'GRAN'POP' must also be mentioned, not only for the escapades of Lawson Wood's worldly-wise ape, but also for

Carreras **Raemaekers War Cartoons** (Black Cat front), 1916 (J, set of 140)

Boguslavsky **Sports Records***, (1 to 25), 1925 (F, set of 25)

BLACK CAT
CIGARETTES

WOOD WORKING.
BOXING & SCREWING UP AMMUNITION BOXES.

12. RIGHT-HAND CROSS COUNTER.

CARRERAS CIGARETTES

Peter Pan.

CLEMATIS

FUDGE WHEEL

the pictures on the reverse of the cards, which featured the firm's newly built Arcadia Factory. Naturally, the cigarette-making machine invented by Bernhard Baron was illustrated along with other processes such as leaf cutting, packing and wrapping.

Just before Baron died in 1929, J A Sinclair of John Sinclair Ltd was appointed a Director of Carreras and shortly afterwards the two businesses became associated. John Sinclair had not been a prolific issuer of cards, although their series of WORLDS COINAGE from 1914 is one of the classic sets. A number of real photographic cards were issued in the 1920s and '30s including 50 ENGLISH & SCOTTISH FOOTBALL STARS and three series of 54 FILM STARS.

In 1937 John Sinclair acquired the business of R J Lea of Stockport. This famous firm had been founded around 1865 and was well known for its Chairman cigarettes. Some excellent cards had been issued by Lea prior to the 1914/18 war, of which the series of CHAIRMAN MINIATURES are outstanding. A further series called MODERN MINIATURES was issued in 1913 in limited numbers but some years later a stock of remainders came onto the market. Unfortunately, four cards were missing so this

set can only usually be collected as a series of 46. No less than 250 cards of OLD POTTERY AND PORCELAIN were issued in five tranches in 1912 and 1913, plus two series of silk cards. They are all most desirable items.

In 1922 a nice set of 25 ENGLISH BIRDS was distributed and the set of 50 ROSES from 1924 compares favourably with the Wills' issues. THE EVOLUTION OF THE ROYAL NAVY was produced the following year and is full of interesting information. From 1934 a number of photographic sets were produced culminating in a series of 54 FAMOUS FILM STARS in 1939. After the 1939/45 conflict the operations of Sinclair and Lea were completely integrated with Carreras.

In 1976, after Carreras themselves had merged with Rothmans Ltd, Black Cat cigarettes were revived and cards were once again issued. Altogether seven series of 50 were produced, similar in size and quality to the standard pre-1940 cards but, sadly, none of the other UK manufacturers followed suit. A further blow was that the cigarettes did not gain a sufficient share of the market and in 1981 it was announced that they and the cards were being withdrawn.

Lea
Left to right:
Chairman Miniatures (Gold Border), 1912 (J, set of 50)
Modern Miniatures, 1913 (G, for 46 cards)
Old Pottery and Porcelain Second Series, 1912 (H, set of 50)
Roses, 1924 (H, set of 50)

page 78
Carreras, *top to bottom*
Left row:
The Science of Boxing (Carreras back), 1920 (J, set of 50)
Figures of Fiction, 1924 (G, set of 25)
History of Army Uniforms, 1937 (G, set of 50)
Middle row:
Races – Historic & Modern, 1927 (G, set of 25)
Right row:
Women on War Work, c1917 (B, per card)
Flowers, 1936 (E, set of 50)
Tools and How to Use Them, 1935 (F, set of 50)

COPE BROS & CO LTD

In 1848 Thomas and George Cope founded another of the major tobacco firms that flourished in Liverpool during the 19th century. When, in 1886, the Government allowed tobacco to be grown in Britain as an experiment, Cope achieved fame by buying up the whole crop. They were also renowned within the trade for their tobacco literature, sponsoring for many years *Tobacco Plant*, a monthly periodical, and also issuing their much prized *Smoke-Room* Booklets. Early cigarette card issues were of the usual actress and beauty types but, true to their literary traditions, they also issued, around 1900, three superb series of CHARACTERS FROM SCOTT, DICKENS' GALLERY and SHAKESPEARE GALLERY.

In 1902 the London firm of Richard Lloyd was acquired. Cope meanwhile continued to produce excellent cards including 25 EMINENT BRITISH REGIMENTS OFFICERS' UNIFORMS, 50 BRITISH WARRIORS, which can be collected with the back printed in black or grey, and a curious set of BOY SCOUTS AND GIRL GUIDES*. A mammoth series of NOTED FOOTBALLERS was also produced, of which 471 cards were issued with Clips

Cope, top to bottom

Left row:
Dickens' Gallery, c1900
(C, per card)

Middle row:
Household Hints, c1925
(H, set of 50)

Right row:
British Warriors (black printing), c1912
(C, per card)

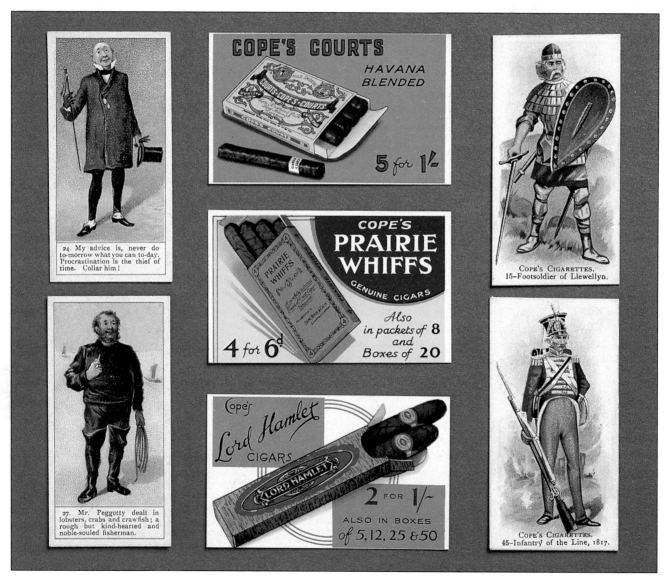

24. My advice is, never do to-morrow what you can to-day. Procrastination is the thief of time. Collar him!

27. Mr. Peggotty dealt in lobsters, crabs and crawfish; a rough but kind-hearted and noble-souled fisherman.

COPE'S COURTS
HAVANA BLENDED
5 for 1/-

COPE'S PRAIRIE WHIFFS
GENUINE CIGARS
4 for 6d
Also in packets of 8 and Boxes of 20

Cope's Lord Hamlet CIGARS
2 for 1/-
ALSO IN BOXES of 5, 12, 25 & 50

COPE'S CIGARETTES.
15-Footsoldier of Llewellyn.

COPE'S CIGARETTES.
45-Infantry of the Line, 1817.

cigarettes, plus another 195 packed with the Solace brand.

After the 1914/18 war Cope produced a series of 32 GOLF STROKES and followed this with 30 LAWN TENNIS STROKES. Both were printed in black and white. Lloyd were more colourful with their 1923 set of 25 OLD ENGLISH INNS and produced a second series in 1924, this time shortening the title to OLD INNS. These issues proved so popular that a further set of 50 was also released. In the late 1920s and early '30s cards were discontinued but when they did reappear there were some choice items for collectors to admire. Among them were ATLANTIC RECORDS from Lloyd, an interesting maritime series, and Cope's THE WORLD'S POLICE. The latter is one of the surprisingly few series featuring the guardians of law and order. For those interested in packaging, a joint issue of HOUSEHOLD HINTS illustrated many of the products marketed by Cope and Lloyd during the years prior to 1940.

In 1939 Cope issued 25 large cards of DICKENS CHARACTER SERIES, which repeated some of the personalities that had featured in their 1900 issue. Then jointly with Lloyd's, two excellent series of CASTLES and CATHEDRALS were distributed, the latter still being inserted through into 1940. After the war the business was acquired by the Gallaher group.

GALLAHER LTD

Tom Gallaher was certainly one of the giants of the tobacco industry. The son of an Irish farmer, he started his own one-man business in 1857 at the age of 17 by making and selling roll pipe tobaccos. In 1863 he had acquired premises in Belfast and a London office followed in 1888. By this time his products included a full range of tobaccos and cigarettes. TYPES OF THE BRITISH ARMY* is thought to be the first set of cards issued in about 1897.

When the ITC was formed in 1901 Tom Gallaher valued his independence too much to be tempted to join. The long series of IRISH VIEW SCENERY issued later stated on the reverse that 'Gallaher Ltd are in NO Ring or Combine'. The famous Park Drive brand was launched and advertisements of the period depicted two

policemen with the caption 'Ten for Two Coppers'. Early card issues included a long series of 111 titled THE SOUTH AFRICAN SERIES and a colourful ROYALTY SERIES to mark the Coronation of King Edward VII. The Newcastle firm of Harvey & Davy was taken over in 1905 and both the acquired and acquirer issued a first class set of 50 BIRDS AND EGGS*.

One of the notable features of most of the cards issued by Gallaher is that their length is marginally shorter and the width slightly larger than the standard size adopted by the ITC branches. Another noticeable fact is that they issued over 30 sets consisting of 100 cards. These can be something of a test for collectors but certainly worth the trouble when the set is as good as WOODLANDS TREES. Another 1912 issue was the 100 card 'SPORTS' SERIES which is an excellent production. During the 1914/18 conflict further lengthy series were issued including, for the practically minded, WHY IS IT? and HOW TO DO IT. But the most memorable wartime sets were the eight series of THE GREAT WAR – VICTORIA CROSS HEROES, each consisting of 25 cards, and the THE GREAT WAR SERIES issued as two sets of 100 cards. One of the many poignant cards is no.169, depicting a cross made of shell cases which marked a French soldier's grave.

Gallaher wasted no time after the war had ended in producing another 100 card series, this time on the more soothing subject of BIRDS, NESTS & EGGS. The 1920s saw the issue of many fine productions including CINEMA STARS and FAMOUS CRICKETERS, and no fewer than four separate series of footballers. BRITISH CHAMPIONS OF 1923 included some rarely recorded pastimes such as Chess, with World Champion Capablanca, and Miss Helen Wilson, the Lady Pipe Player of Scotland.

During the coupon war of the early '30s Gallaher turned their back on card issues but when, by agreement, this form of promotion was discontinued, they certainly made up for lost time.

Tom Gallaher founder of Gallaher Ltd

Gallaher **Irish View Scenery**, c1908 (A, per card)

Gallaher **The Great War Second Series**, 1916 (K, set of 100)

CORPORAL,
CAMERONIANS,
SCOTTISH RIFLES.

GALLAHER'S

CIGARETTES

Gallaher's Cigarettes

J.R.CAPABLANCA.

ROYALTY SERIES No 34

Princess
VICTORIA OF WALES.

WHY
can flies walk on the ceiling?

GALLAHER'S
CIGARETTES

A House Fly's
leg greatly enlarged

2nd-Lieut. G. T. DORRELL. V.C.

Daimler

DAIMLER "15" SPORTS COUPE

WALL

TIGER MOTH

HUGH GALLACHER
NEWCASTLE UNITED

GRETA GARBO
(M-G-M)

S. DONOGHUE

POLAR BEAR

One of the best sets of MOTOR CARS was issued in 1934, but, sadly, only in a series of 24 cards. The more familiar sets of 48 cards, printed by the offset litho process, also appeared at this time. CHAMPIONS OF SCREEN & STAGE featured the likes of Garbo, Crawford and Gable, whereas the set with the simple title CHAMPIONS pictured the sporting celebrities of the day.

In September 1934 it was announced that Gallaher had acquired the International Tobacco Co Ltd with their Summit brand and also Peter Jackson, proprietors of perhaps the most famous of pre-war filter tip cigarettes, Du Maurier. International issued only one set of traditional cards in the home market but that was a very interesting set of 50 INTERNATIONAL CODE OF SIGNALS. It was not long before Gallaher were on the take-over trail again and this time they bought control of E Robinson & Sons of Stockport, who had themselves within the previous few years acquired Illingworth of Kendal and the Manchester based business of J A Pattreiouex Ltd.

Illingworth, which was founded in 1867, had previously issued cards including two interesting and original sets of MOTOR CAR BONNETS* and 'COMICARTOONS' OF SPORT. Pattreiouex could date their origins back to 1861 when 24 year old Joseph A Pattreiouex started manufacturing tobacco. One of their best selling brands was Junior Member, named after the first grandchild

of the founder. Pattreiouex had started issuing cards in the 1920s and had concentrated on photographic issues, including 96 FAMOUS CRICKETERS and many series of footballers. Several scenic cards were also produced in both large and standard sizes but in view of the variety of different printings the sets are not easy to complete.

Pattreiouex also issued the more conventional letterpress cards, one of the best sets being BUILDERS OF THE BRITISH EMPIRE. The Senior Service brand had been introduced before the business passed to Robinson and had met with moderate success. When the price was switched to 10 for 6d and a new type of medium sized photographic card was issued, sales really started to escalate. Among many fine insertions with this brand were SIGHTS OF LONDON, SIGHTS OF BRITAIN, COASTWISE and BEAUTIFUL SCOTLAND. A series on THE NAVY also appeared plus an excellent set on BRITISH RAILWAYS. After the acquisition by Gallaher, some of these items were also packed with Gallaher, Illingworth and Peter Jackson brands.

Gallaher, meanwhile, were getting a favourable reaction of their own with several attractive series of small cards. After concentrating on film and sporting celebrities in 1936 and 1937, BRITISH BIRDS, WILD ANIMALS, TRAINS OF THE WORLD and BUTTERFLIES AND MOTHS made a welcome change. With war clouds gathering AEROPLANES and ARMY BADGES were among the last sets to be issued. Shortly after the 1939/45 war had ended, the business of J R Freeman was acquired and this was followed by Cope in 1953. Gallaher finally lost its own independence when American Brands took a 67% stake in 1968, subsequently extended to 100% in 1975.

International **International Code of Signals**, 1934 (E, set of 50)

Gallaher **Trains of the World**, 1937 (F, set of 48)

R & J HILL LTD

This firm can trace its foundation back to Shoreditch in 1775, when the brothers Hill started manufacturing tobacco. One brother had two sons, Robert and James, who took over the business and when they died the firm became a limited company in 1871. The first cards to be issued were probably the STATUARY* series, which were advertised to appear in a new Fine Art brand of cigarettes in January 1899. Some series of actresses were distributed and also the popular set of COLONIAL TROOPS*, which appeared with three different advertisement backs. BATTLESHIPS AND CRESTS* from around 1901 are superb cards which do not, fortunately, suffer from this complication.

In 1905 Hill acquired the well-established firm of Henry Archer & Co, who had themselves issued cards of the familiar actress and beauty type. At about this time Hill were packing a JAPANESE SERIES*, which featured some of the personalities of the Russo-Japanese War. In 1912, a FAMOUS CRICKETERS SERIES was distributed, to mark the triangular tournament

played that summer between England, Australia and South Africa. A NATIONAL FLAG SERIES was put out in 1914, as was a set of 20 TYPES OF THE BRITISH ARMY. Hill's most famous wartime issue was titled FRAGMENTS FROM FRANCE and featured the wonderful cartoons created by Bruce Bairnsfather for *The Bystander*.

Sports fans were no doubt pleased in 1923 when card issues resumed, as sets of both FAMOUS CRICKETERS and FAMOUS FOOTBALLERS were issued in that year. A more unusual series was a set of 84 WIRELESS TELEPHONY, possibly issued as a result of the first broadcast by the newly-formed BBC. The centenary of the railway was marked in 1925 by the issue of two series in both standard and large sized cards. MUSIC HALL CELEBRITIES – PAST & PRESENT appeared in 1930 with Little Tich and Marie Lloyd among those representing the past and the inimitable Will Hay and Lancashire's own Gracie Fields taking care of the present.

Tricks and puzzles have always been a popular topic for cards and Hill's PUZZLE SERIES is as good as any. During the 1930s the cinema was overdone as a subject but FAMOUS FILM STARS and the series of 40 SCENES FROM THE FILMS are nice black and white studies which feature many of the less well-known artistes of the day. In 1938 Hill started issuing a series of large, hand-coloured photographic VIEWS OF INTEREST with their Spinet and Sunripe brands. These proved to be hugely popular with collectors and eventually ran to five series. Similarly styled sets for Canada and India followed in 1940 but the latter were quickly discontinued due to the war and are today quite hard to find.

---

page 84, left to right

Hill

Top row:
Colonial Troops*, c1901 (E, per card)
Battleships and Crests*, c1901 (D, per card)
Types of the British Army, 1914 (F, per card)
Fragments from France (coloured), 1916 (E, per card)

Bottom row:
Music Hall Celebrities – Past & Present, 1930 (G, set of 30)
Famous Film Stars, 1938 (F, set of 40)
Puzzle Series, 1937 (G, set of 50)
Wireless Telephony, 1923 (I, set of 84)

The Hill factory premises were completely destroyed due to enemy action in 1941 and any remainders, plus the company records, all perished. After the war the company stayed independent until 1953 when the shares were purchased by the John Sinclair branch of Carreras.

GODFREY PHILLIPS LTD

Founded in 1844 by a young man of 18 the business eventually became extremely successful. Not only was the firm a prolific producer of cards and silks, it also had a penchant for acquiring or controlling other tobacco manufacturers and merchants. The Cartophilic Society's *Reference Book No.13* gives a short biography of the company and lists 24 other businesses, which by 1948 had been absorbed or were operating as subsidiaries.

Among the earliest card issues are a GENERAL INTEREST* series and several sets featuring anonymous pin-up girls of the day. TYPES OF BRITISH AND COLONIAL TROOPS* was issued during the Boer War and in 1904 25 BOXER REBELLION* cards were distributed. Also about the time of the Boer War Phillips issued some black and white cards, mainly of celebrities, inscribed Guinea Gold Cigarettes. These can be confusing to collectors as many associate this brand only with Ogden's. In fact, Phillips used the same brand name for some years before eventually withdrawing it from the market.

Unlike many houses, which moved away from cards of 'beauties' during the Edwardian period, Phillips kept up a steady stream of these issues through to World War I. Some were titled, such as the attractive photos of BRITISH BEAUTIES, and others have been given adopted titles. All tastes were, however, catered for with an extremely fine INDIAN SERIES of 25 coloured cards and a lovely CHINESE SERIES*. The latter has a statement on the reverse that the pictures were drawn by a Chinese artist of high repute. For nature lovers the ANIMAL SERIES, BRITISH BUTTERFLIES NO. 1 ISSUE and EGGS, NESTS & BIRDS all provide lots of interest.

During the first decade of the 20th century Phillips started on the acquisition trail and snapped up the well-established firm of W J

Hill **Japanese Series***
(coloured, red panel), 1904
(G, per card)

Phillips **General Interest***,
c1895 (G, per card)

PHILLIPS' CIGARETTES

IBEX.

MAJOR-GENERAL STOESSEL.
Commands Russian Forces at Tientsin.
Phillips' Cigarettes.

西蜀宮女任氏

INDIAN SERIES No 9

STREET IN PESHAWUR

PEACOCK.

Nora Wadeley.

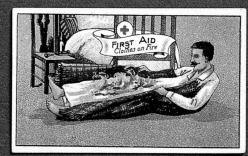

FIRST AID
Clothes on Fire

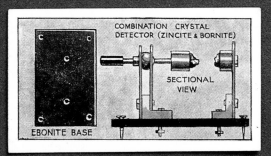

COMBINATION CRYSTAL
DETECTOR (ZINCITE & BORNITE)

SECTIONAL
VIEW

EBONITE BASE

HEMPHILL SCHOOLS Waukesha Diesel

DIESEL CAR

MICHELANGELO

ORANDO LABORANDO

RUGBY

H. CARTER

Harris & Son. Harris had previously produced cards and an associate, Moustafa & Co, was to issue five series under its own name in the 1920s. With the advent of war there was no lessening in the quality of cards produced, of which the FIRST AID SERIES and MORSE SIGNALLING are good examples. Of the cards more directly related to the war, the real photos of BRITISH WARSHIPS are particularly atmospheric.

From 1922 many interesting and unusual series were produced but mention must be made of the miniature size photographic cards of cricketers and footballers that were issued with Pinnace cigarettes. For over 70 years these have given collectors much pleasure, plus a measure of frustration, in the continuing struggle to achieve complete sets of the many hundreds of cards issued. At the time, 25 of the small cards could be exchanged for a large cabinet sized photo, and although these premium cards were not inserted in packets they are eagerly sought after today. The cricketers are particularly hard to find. Other interesting sets from the 1920s are DERBY WINNERS & JOCKEYS, RED INDIANS, FAMOUS BOYS and MODEL RAILWAYS. For early radio buffs there were also sets on HOW TO MAKE YOUR OWN WIRELESS SET, HOW TO MAKE A VALVE AMPLIFIER and finally, HOW TO BUILD A TWO VALVE SET.

---

page 86, left to right
Phillips
First row:
Animal Series, c1903 (B, per card)
Boxer Rebellion, 1904 (E, per card)
Chinese Series*, c1910 (J, set of 25)
Indian Series, 1908 (D, per card)
Second row:
British Butterflies No.1 Issue, 1911 (J, set of 30)
British Beauties (55-108), 1915 (J, set of 54)
First Aid Series, 1914 (J, set of 25)
Third row:
How to Make Your Own Wireless Set, 1923 (G, set of 25)
This Mechanised Age First Series (adhesive), 1936 (C, set of 50)
Fourth row:
Famous Minors, 1936 (C, set of 50)
School Badges, 1927 (F, set of 25)
Soccer Stars, 1936 (G, set of 50)
Model Railways, 1927 (H, set of 25)

As the 1920s progressed Phillips added to their organisation a number of important houses and brands – Cavanders, J Millhoff with their famous De Reszke cigarettes, and Abdullah & Co. Cavanders could trace their history back to 1775 but were not known as card issuers until 1924. They produced a profusion of series from the mid-1920s, many of them being photographic and camera studies. Millhoff was of more recent inception, but once part of the Phillips' group they also issued a fair quantity of cards. Some were photographic and those of FAMOUS GOLFERS and FAMOUS 'TEST' CRICKETERS are keenly sought after. Their two large card series of ENGLAND, HISTORIC & PICTURESQUE are quietly attractive with pastel type colours. Abdullah had quickly built up a good reputation since being founded in 1902. Most of their cards were issued in export brands and there were some interesting German language cards which were discontinued once that branch was closed in 1934.

In 1929 the shares of Cohen Weenen & Co Ltd were purchased and through them came control of the United Kingdom Tobacco Co Ltd. The latter in turn owned Major Drapkin, Nicholas Sarony, Marcovitch and Muratti, who all had issued, or were to issue, cards. Cohen Weenen had been founded in 1864 and for the first 25 years of their existence had concentrated on cigars. They issued a number of cards around the turn of the century including CELEBRITIES*, of which several series and sub series appeared. Sport was also a popular theme with FOOTBALL CAPTAINS, HEROES OF SPORT*, FAMOUS BOXERS* and OWNERS, JOCKEYS, FOOTBALLERS, CRICKETERS being among the series issued. During the 1914/18 conflict a WAR SERIES* was distributed plus a further 50 cards covering VC HEROES*. In 1923 two pre-war series of NATIONS and WONDERS OF THE WORLD were reissued and there followed a nice monochrome series of CRICKETERS*. Disappointingly, no cards were produced after the acquisition by Phillips.

A number of shared series were issued during the '30s, such as BRITISH BUTTERFLIES and OLD FAVOURITES from Phillips and Abdullah, FEATHERED FRIENDS from Phillips, Abdullah and

Phillips **Footballers***
(Pinnace 1-940), c1923
(A, per card)

Millhoff **Famous Golfers**,
1928 (C, per card)

Col. HALL WALKER M. CANNON. JOUBERT F. H. HUISH.

Cohen Weenen
Owners, Jockeys,
Footballers, Cricketers,
c1906 (C, per card)

Cavanders, SCHOOL BADGES from Phillips and Cavanders and AIRCRAFT and BRITISH ORDERS OF CHIVALRY & VALOUR from both Phillips and United Kingdom Tobacco. There were also plenty of individual issues from Phillips and the associated companies. FAMOUS MINORS is a series of 50 devoted to those who made their mark before attaining their majority. In this set we can find Mozart, Michelangelo and Marco Polo. For royalty enthusiasts the SPECIAL JUBILEE YEAR SERIES reviewed the reign of King George V and was issued in medium and postcard sizes.

Football fans need to exercise care when collecting FAMOUS FOOTBALLERS, INTERNATIONAL CAPS and SOCCER STARS, as there is considerable duplication of portraiture, especially between the first two sets named. The first series of THIS MECHANISED AGE was a colourful and interesting set put out in 1936 with both adhesive and non-adhesive backs. The value to collectors in having the non-adhesive back is reflected in the catalogue valuations which differ by £3 or £4. In a way the Phillips issues ended much as they began, as in 1938 they started a long running series of BEAUTIES OF TO-DAY. These glossy photos were appearing in packets as the curtain came down on cigarette cards. Phillips remained a major independent company until about 1968 when Philip Morris took a controlling interest.

S. MATTHEWS

Phillips **Famous Footballers**,
1936 (G, set of 50)

JAMES TADDY & CO

When mention is made of this august firm there is a tendency to speak in hushed tones, such is their reputation. They certainly did produce some wonderful cards and their best are unsurpassed. But there were some fairly ordinary ones as well. The quality of the cards is not the only reason for the mystical appeal of the 'Taddy' name. Another important factor is the bizarre circumstances in which this traditional firm closed down its business in 1920. In terms of age they were one of the senior tobacco houses, having been founded in 1740. The firm took premises in the Minories around 1855 and over the years built up a loyal clientele. Cards appeared towards the end of the 19th century and the first two series were probably ENGLISH ROYALTY* and ACTRESSES*, both printed by the collotype process.

NATIVES OF THE WORLD* and the KLONDYKE SERIES were produced in colour just prior to 1900, the latter marking the famous gold rush of 1896. The Boer War was the catalyst for six series of VICTORIA CROSS HEROES which totalled 125 cards in all. Other beautifully lithographed cards from this period include the THAMES SERIES, RUSSO-JAPANESE WAR* and the 'ROYALTY' SERIES. From 1907 two long running series of PROMINENT FOOTBALLERS and COUNTY

CRICKETERS were distributed, the former being issued in three tranches through to the 1913-14 season. All these cards, and two series marking the tours to Britain of the South African cricket and football teams, were printed in monochrome. A superb 'HERALDRY' SERIES was issued in full colour around 1913 and featured the arms of 25 Dukes. A year or two earlier Taddy had distributed two series of 25 ORDERS OF CHIVALRY, which were equally handsome.

There is, however, one set of 20 cards that is not particularly well printed, has plain backs,

Taddy

Left to right, top row:
Klondyke Series, c1900 (G, per card)
Boer Leaders, c1900 (D, per card)
VC Heroes – Boer War (61-80), c1900 (D, per card)
'Royalty' Series, c1908 (D, per card)

Bottom row:
Orders of Chivalry (1st Series), c1911 (D, per card)
Prominent Footballers (with footnote), 1908 (C, per card)
County Cricketers, 1907 (G, per card)
Russo-Japanese War* (26-50), 1904 (E, per card)

Taddy 'Heraldry' Series,
c1911 (D, per card)

Taddy Clowns and Circus
Artistes*, unissued
(K, per card)

was probably never officially issued, yet makes the headlines when it comes up for sale at auction. Known as CLOWNS AND CIRCUS ARTISTES* these cards have come to represent the ultimate dream of most British card collectors. Possibly the full story about them will never be known but the most popular theory is that the cards were proofs of a new issue about to be printed when the firm suddenly closed down in 1920. How that particular tragedy came about is well known. Tobacco workers were called upon by their Union to strike in order to win more pay and better working conditions. Although Taddy's operatives were non-union and paid above union rates, the workforce decided to strike in sympathy. The management warned that if the strike went ahead they would close the business down for good.

Presumably, the threat was not taken seriously. In any event the workforce withdrew their labour and the factory gates were closed forever. Long service office staff were pensioned off and subsequent offers for the goodwill of the business were all refused. There is a postscript to this sad event in that 60 years later a new Taddy company was formed, issuing cards principally for framing. Advertisements implied

that these were original items but upon a complaint being upheld by the Advertising Standards Authority the sponsors ceased trading.

THE MINOR TOBACCO COMPANIES

The heading is a little unfair on companies such as B Morris & Sons, Murray, Sons & Co and J Wix & Sons who were all substantial companies and issued many fine card series. In fact, Morris were one of the first firms to issue cards in the UK when they distributed their BEAUTIES – COLLOTYPE* in the 1890s. These cards are virtually impossible to find but a later series of 30 ACTRESSES*, issued in black and white, can be purchased very reasonably due to a stock of remainders being acquired by a leading dealing house in the 1940s. Two series were issued in connection with the South African War, including a fine coloured BOER WAR, 1900 issue. During the First World War Morris issued 25 WAR CELEBRITIES in gravure and two coloured series of WAR PICTURES and NATIONAL & COLONIAL ARMS. In the period between the wars some well-produced cards appeared including MEASUREMENT OF TIME, GOLF STROKES, HOW TO SKETCH and the fascinating production of HOW FILMS ARE MADE.

Murray, like Morris, were founded in 1810 but it was not until 1888 that the Belfast-based firm extended their operations to the mainland. An ACTRESSES* series and some sepia pictures of IRISH SCENERY* were among the earliest issues. PROMINENT POLITICIANS were packed with Front Bench cigarettes and subsequent issues included footballers, cricketers and even polo players. BATHING BEAUTIES, CINEMA SCENES and DANCING GIRLS were photographic sets which all appeared in 1929 and, to provide some variety, TYPES OF AEROPLANES was also issued that year. THE STORY OF SHIPS was released in 1940 and this attractive set is still available at a modest cost.

Julius Wix was a tobacco blender of some note who eventually set up his own business in 1898. After World War I the Kensitas brand gained great popularity but the firm was more renowned for its coupon schemes than for cigarette cards. In 1927 the American Tobacco Company acquired control and cards started to appear. The mischievous HENRY, drawn by artist Carl Anderson, featured in several series from 1935 and in 1937 two colourful sets were distributed titled CORONATION and BUILDERS OF EMPIRE. Advertisements between the wars had featured Jenkyns, the archetypal butler, and several cards were issued, known as JENKYNISMS*, quoting his pithy sayings.

One of the pioneer tobacco firms was E & W Anstie of Devizes, who are thought to have been manufacturing snuff in 1698. Most of their cards were issued during the inter-war period, including a colourful SCOUT SERIES. They were also noted for their many fine sectional series. The business of I Rutter & Co was acquired in 1925 and this old established firm had issued several series around the turn of the century, including a scarce CRICKETERS SERIES and COMIC PHRASES*. Anstie was itself bought by the ITC in 1944.

Other firms were absorbed by the ITC as a consequence of having well-established retail outlets and among them were A Baker & Co and Salmon & Gluckstein. The former issued a small number of actress and beauty sets between 1898 and 1902 but Salmon & Gluckstein had a more ambitious issuing policy. All their cards appeared prior to 1917 apart from a couple of later series. Among the best are CHARACTERS FROM DICKENS*, SHAKESPEARIAN SERIES, THE POST IN VARIOUS COUNTRIES* and 'OWNERS & JOCKEYS' SERIES.

The Co-operative Wholesale Society and the Scottish CWS both issued cards, although most appeared after the 1914/18 war. The latter, as might be expected, produced a nice set of 25 on BURNS and also an attractive series of DWELLINGS

Salmon & Gluckstein
'Owners & Jockeys' Series, c1902 (G, per card)

Morris **Measurement of Time**, 1924 (F, set of 25)

Top to bottom

Left row:
Anstie **Scout Series**, 1923 (I, set of 50)
Scottish CWS **Dwellings of all Nations**
(small numerals), 1924 (I, set of 25)

Middle row:
Morris **How Films Are Made**, 1934 (F, set of 25)

Wix **Jenkynisms*** (2nd Series),1932 (G, set of 50 large)
Amalgamated Tobacco Corporation **Interesting Hobbies**,
1959 (C, set of 25)

Right row:
Salmon & Gluckstein **Shakespearian Series**
(with frame), c1899 (F, per card)
CWS **Western Stars**, 1957 (C, set of 24)

OF ALL NATIONS. The English branch, whose most famous pre-1918 issue was an unusual PARROT SERIES, put out more than a dozen series between the wars. Their WAYSIDE FLOWERS and FAMOUS BUILDINGS are better than many other series on these subjects. They were one of very few firms to issue cards after 1940, as in 1957 they packed WESTERN STARS with their Jaycee Tipped cigarettes. This set gives a rare chance to obtain cards of such stalwart actors as Ernest Borgnine, Ward Bond and Forrest Tucker.

Another firm that used cigarette cards after the 1939/45 war was Phillip Allman & Co, who issued a CORONATION SERIES to mark the accession to the throne of Queen Elizabeth II. But by far the main issuer of cards in this period was the company Allman became associated with, Amalgamated Tobacco Corporation. They only issued a handful of sets directly within the UK but their export issues are widely available to collectors. One of the 1959 issues was INTERESTING HOBBIES, which naturally included cigarette card collecting.

There were close to 300 British firms who issued cards, of which about 100 never got

Anglo Cigarette **Tariff Reform Series**, 1909 (F, per card)

beyond a first series. One of the more interesting of these was the Anglo Cigarette Manufacturing Co, who issued a TARIFF REFORM SERIES with their 'Tariff Reform' brand of cigarettes in 1909. Cards dealing with political issues are rare and this set covered one of the contentious matters on which the 1910 election was fought. Questions were raised in Parliament as to whether the Conservatives were funding the issue but this accusation was proved to be without foundation. In the event the Liberals were returned to power and the cigarettes were withdrawn. The manufacturers, however, are still active today in a different form as Molins, a leading producer of tobacco equipment.

NICE.

Richmond, ALLEN & GINTER'S Virginia
CIGARETTES

Narragansett Pier.

He stoops to conquer.

FORGET ME NOT   AUSTRIA

Hedgehog

FIRST QUARTER

10

พระรถโยนสาร

ENRICO CARUSO.

CHAPTER 7

COLLECTING WORLDWIDE

Cigarette cards have appeared in packets in most parts of the world at one time or another. As might be expected, where a state monopoly controlled the local tobacco industry, picture cards, which are after all advertisements, were not generally used. Cigarette cards are thought to have originated in North America but once the American Tobacco Company had been broken up by the Federal Government in 1911 the flow of cards reduced significantly. Then in 1915 a combination of circumstances, including a switch to a soft 'cup' type packet which made card insertion difficult, led to the abandonment of cards. This helps to explain why the American collecting market developed in an entirely different way to that in the UK.

So far as cigarette cards are concerned, British collectors have never shown much enthusiasm for foreign card issues. Obviously, the language barrier is one deterrent where cards are produced in non-English speaking countries. Another is that a large number of the issues, particularly from Australia and New Zealand, mirror cards put out in the home market. Also, there is a touch of natural British conservatism which means collectors are unwilling to experiment with overseas cards which can come in a variety of shapes, sizes and formats. This chapter will, therefore, concentrate on those countries where cards are reasonably available to British collectors. A separate section is devoted to BAT, as many of their cards do not specify the countries in which they were issued.

THE AMERICAS

In 1890 the five largest cigarette manufacturers in the USA joined together to form the American Tobacco Company. These were Allen & Ginter, W Duke, Sons & Co, Goodwin & Co, Wm S Kimball and Kinney Bros. All issued cards under their own name prior to the merger but after that date, cards were either issued under the banner of the ATC, or indicated that the firm was part of the ATC. Other acquisitions were made and by 1900 it was estimated that over 90% of all domestic cigarette manufacture was controlled by this giant organisation.

Early American cards concentrated heavily on the female face and figure. Some were photographic cards but many were lithographed on thick board and are among the most delightful representations of this art form. So popular were cards of actresses and show-girls that when in 1880 Thos H Hall of New York issued four PRESIDENTIAL CANDIDATE* cards, this short series was completed by the addition of

---

page 94, top to bottom

Left row:
Allen & Ginter **City Flags**, c1888 (C, per card)
American Tobacco Co **National Flags and Flowers – Girls***, c1900 (D, per card)
BAT **Siamese Dancers***, c1915 (G, set of 50)

Middle row:
Kimball **Beautiful Bathers**, c1889
(F, per extra large card)

Ogden's Ruler (BAT) **Animals***, c1912 (J, set of 60)
UTC **Our South African National Parks**, 1941
(D, set of 100 medium)

Right row:
Duke **Jokes**, c1890 (D, per card)
BAT **Beauties – Marine and Universe Girls***, c1903
(C, per card)
Scerri **Prominent People**, c1930 (A, per card)

Cohasset

Portugese

Left:
Kimball **Fancy Bathers**,
c1889 (D, per card)
Right:
Kimball **Dancing Women**,
c1889 (D, per card)

Duke **State Governors, Coats of Arms, etc*** (Folders),
c1888 (D, per card)

We are the largest Cigarette Manufacturers in the World.

GOV. STEVENSON, IDAHO TER.
TURKISH CROSS-CUT CIGARETTES
ARE THE BEST.
W. Duke Sons & Co
DURHAM, N.C. & NEW YORK.

Our average sales are over
TWO MILLIONS PER DAY.

four actresses. This set is one of the earliest that can be definitively dated. Many other series, including Allen & Ginter's PARASOL DRILL, Duke's MUSICAL INSTRUMENTS and Kinney's FAMOUS GEMS OF THE WORLD are little more than an excuse to picture a pretty girl.

At least with Kimball's DANCING WOMEN and FANCY BATHERS the collector has a good idea of what to expect!

Another feature of these early US cards is that, although unnumbered, they were often 'backlisted'. This meant that the title of each card in the series was printed on the back as an aid to collectors. This did have the disadvantage that no text could be included but in some series, such as Duke's HOLIDAYS and VEHICLES OF THE WORLD, descriptive matter was printed in place of the backlisting.

There were also a significant number of extra large cards issued, mostly for distribution in 50 or 100 packings and perhaps even for use as premium issues. Many featured the usual pretty girls, such as GEMS OF BEAUTY from Duke, but others covered a variety of subjects including the

same issuer's BREEDS OF HORSES*, COWBOY SCENES and an unusual triptych design for STATE GOVERNORS, COATS OF ARMS & MAPS*.

Some interesting population figures are given on the back of that series based on the census for 1880. At that time Idaho had a total population of 32,610, little more than 10% of tiny Rhode Island, smallest of the then 38 States. Allen & Ginter produced a similar set in standard size, titled FLAGS OF THE STATES AND TERRITORIES, but then extended the format with two series of FLAGS OF ALL NATIONS. The same firm put out an attractive set of 50 CELEBRATED AMERICAN INDIAN CHIEFS, which included the distinguished features of Crow's Breast, Grey Eagle and Red Cloud. There were some equally noteworthy portraits presented in Consolidated Cigarette's LADIES OF THE WHITE HOUSE and America's predilection for sport made Goodwin's CHAMPIONS and GAMES AND SPORTS SERIES deservedly popular.

Prior to the Tobacco War and the formation of BAT there had been an active export drive by American producers. We have already seen that Allen & Ginter were marketing their cigarettes in the UK in the 1880s but the main growth in exports occurred after the formation of the ATC and the elimination of any serious domestic competition. All continents were targeted but a significant impression was made in Japan and the Far East through Murai Bros and in Australia, where local subsidiaries were established. Most of the cards found in the UK were issued during the Tobacco War and commonly feature actresses, beauties and Boer War celebrities. Some of the cards show on the back the name of the ATC brand whilst others refer simply to the American Tobacco Co, either in plain type or within a criss-cross net design.

In the first years of the new century, card issues within the US became increasingly augmented by novelties such as mini rugs and blankets, buttons, silks and leather items. The considerable expense of these give-aways probably helped to hasten the demise of promotional inserts in 1915. There was a minor resurgence of card interest in the 1930s, including a series on HENRY, using some of the same designs that were currently being issued in the UK by J Wix & Sons.

In Canada cigarette cards never caught on to the same extent. US cigarettes were sold widely across the border and one of the main local companies, D Ritchie & Co, was taken over by the ATC in the 1890s. The Imperial Tobacco Company of Canada Ltd was formed under the control of BAT late in 1902 and cards were issued spasmodically until the Great War sparked off the production of several military sets. Some of these were similar to UK issues put out by the ITC branches but VICTORIA CROSS HEROES was purely for overseas. During the inter-war period there was again a mixture of original items and others based on UK designs.

Cuba was the one export market that remained with the ATC after the formation of BAT in 1902. The main local producer was the firm of Henry Clay and Bock and they produced many photographic series, often quoting the Susini brand. Another Havana producer was Diaz and one of their series was in the form of a miniature postcard. This, in fact, was a fairly popular format in the region. Throughout most of South America cards were popular at one time or another. Venezuela, Peru, Chile and Argentina all produced a fair number of series which invariably consisted of glossy photos.

AUSTRALASIA

Prior to 1902 both the ATC and the major British houses made determined efforts to woo the Australian and New Zealand smokers. Ogden's cards and cigarettes were among those distributed in Australia through the firm's Sydney branch around the time of the Tobacco War. After the formation of BAT the main local competition in Australia was provided by Sniders & Abrahams, who issued cards from 1904 until about 1917. The largest part of their output was related to Australian football and horse racing. Another Australian passion, cricket, was also catered for including a set of 40 CRICKETERS IN ACTION*. After the 1914/18 conflict, the firm of J J Schuh issued some more footballers and jockeys, before they too disappeared from the scene.

Using the Wills name but without the ITC Clause, BAT issued many fine series in Australia. The main brands used were Capstan, Havelock and Vice Regal and often the same series is collectable in all three brands. Many UK series were released, although not all had been originally issued by the Wills branch. A TOUR ROUND THE WORLD and ARMS & ARMOUR are examples. Some of the issues, such as 'MERRIE ENGLAND' STUDIES based on sketches by the

Henry Clay and Bock
Alrededor Del Mundo,
c1910 (A, per card)

Sniders & Abrahams
Cricketers in Action*, c1906
(G, per card)

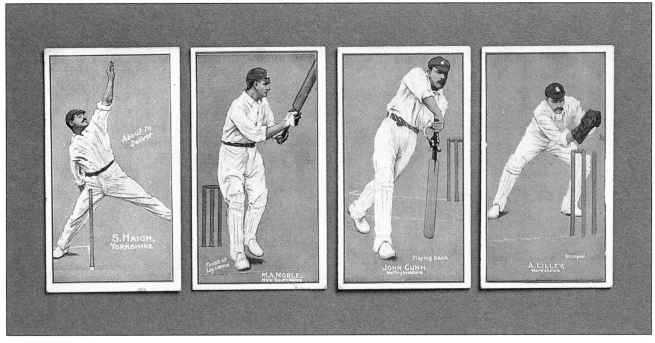

Wills (BAT) **'Merrie England'**
Studies, c1916 (B, per card)

artist John Hassall, were produced for general distribution by BAT but there were, of course, many items geared directly to the Australian market. AUSTRALIAN WILD FLOWERS and BIRDS OF AUSTRALASIA are two examples and, inevitably , there were also several cricket sets produced.

Godfrey Phillips had an active Australian subsidiary which issued cards in the 1930s, concentrating mainly on the 'safe' subjects of footballers, cricketers and sporting celebrities. Carreras was another to take an interest in this market by purchasing the business of G G Goode.

In New Zealand, no local tobacco industry seemed to develop to challenge the marketing skills of the ATC and BAT. So once the early diet of beauties and actresses dried up, no cards were recorded until Ardath's wartime export issues. In the 1920s Ardath resumed card issues and, with the Wills' brands, BAT also issued NEW ZEALAND BIRDS and NZ BUTTERFLIES, MOTHS &

BEETLES. The Lambert & Butler and John Player brands were also sold by BAT in New Zealand and an example of the inserts packed with the latter's cigarettes is WHALING, which appeared in 1930.

Godfrey Phillips group were among others who exported to New Zealand but mostly their cards are not distinguishable from the home issues. One exception was the set of ANNUALS, where Phillips had to change the text to reflect the different growing seasons. J Wix made a special series titled ROYAL TOUR IN NEW ZEALAND and several of the Ardath home issues appeared but with non-adhesive backs. One local company was formed, in association with BAT, called Dominion Tobacco, with the idea of exploiting the home-grown tobacco crop. Four series of cards were issued from the mid '20s before the company decided the experiment was not worth pursuing.

Player (BAT) **Whaling**, c1930
(G, set of 25)

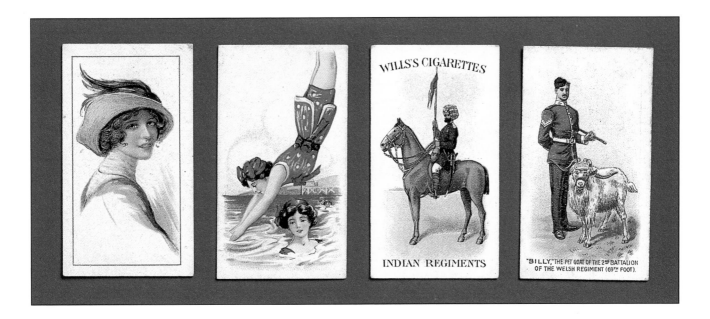

MIDDLE EAST AND ASIA

Quite a few companies issued cards in Egypt, although these were mainly confined to a ten-year period prior to 1915. The majority of these series are photographic and feature beauties, children and occasionally, celebrities or scenes. Cards were probably packed for the benefit of tourists and those issued by Stamelis Douras and E D Protopapas do crop up from time to time. Maspero Freres of Jaffa were associated with BAT and issued a coloured series of BIRDS, BEASTS AND FISHES during the 1920s.

As might be expected, British firms were strongly represented in India from an early date. No doubt export packs contained cards and in addition issues were made through companies such as Planters Stores of Calcutta and The Star Tobacco Co of Bombay. The cards most frequently found, however, are those issued by BAT through the Wills Scissors brand. BEAUTIES – PICTURE HATS* and SPORTING GIRLS* are typical of the many cards which featured the fairer sex. The DERBY DAY SERIES was a 25 card sectional set and would have given expatriates a reminder of one of the top sporting events back home. That the cigarettes were geared towards service personnel is confirmed by a number of series, including INDIAN REGIMENTS and REGIMENTAL COLOURS AND CAP BADGES*. This latter states on

the back that the cigarettes were of a 'Special Army Quality'. Ogden's Ruler was another brand used by BAT in India and a set of 60 ANIMALS* was issued there in 1912.

BAT were also very strongly established in Thailand, or Siam as it was called before 1939. Teal and Eagle Bird cigarettes were the brands mainly used and the latter's different sets of Siamese plays are very attractive. Also worth looking out for are the series of SIAMESE HOROSCOPES* and SIAMESE UNIFORMS*. Malaysia and Indonesia were among the many countries where BAT had influence but the biggest market was that of pre-Communist China. Several different brands were used within this market and CHINESE HEROES* and CHINESE TRADES* were among those series issued with Pinhead cigarettes. Wills' Pirate brand was another used and CHINA'S FAMOUS WARRIORS* was a colourful issue inserted with these cigarettes . As was the case with many of the cards produced for eastern markets, the reverse merely shows an illustration of the packet.

Prior to BAT's formation, the Egyptian Cigarettes Manufacturing Co of Shanghai had issued a few series with English language backs, including ARMIES OF THE WORLD* and TYPES OF BRITISH AND COLONIAL TROOPS*. Very

Wills Scissors (BAT)
Left to right:
Beauties – Picture Hats*, c1914 (I, set of 32)
Sporting Girls*, c1910 (K, set of 30)
Indian Regiments Series, 1910 (B, per card)
Regimental Pets*, c1910 (B, per card)

Stamelis Douras **Photo Series 1***, c1905 (C, per card)

BAT (Eagle Bird Brand)

Left to right, top row:
Siamese Horoscopes*,
c1916 (G, set of 50)

Bottom row:
**Siamese Play – Khun Chang
Khun Phaen I***, c1917
(G, set of 50)

Right:
Nanyang Bros **Weapons of
War***, c1935
(G, set of 40 medium)

active in China and other parts of the Far East was the firm of Nanyang Brothers, and their cards often have the initials 'NY' on the reverse. Many other Chinese firms issued cards and Foh Chong, Hwa Ching and Kiu Cheong are just three examples. In Japan, Murai Bros were the most prolific issuers. From 1895 to 1902 they were owned by the ATC and then briefly by BAT. WORLD'S SMOKERS* is an example from the ATC period with ACTRESSES 'ALWICS'* being one the series distributed through BAT.

SOUTH AFRICA

Although it is possible to find cards that were issued in North and Central Africa the main area of interest for cartophilists is within South Africa. Sales of both American and British cigarettes can be dated back to the 1890s and there were also some local manufacturers who were issuing cards. Wills produced local issues as did Taddy. The latter's ADMIRALS & GENERALS – THE WAR actually quotes a Cape Town address. Card issues were, however, few and far between until BAT, through their subsidiary United Tobacco Companies (UTC), became more active in the 1920-1940 period. The main local competition was provided by African Tobacco Manufacturers (AMT) but they were eventually acquired by UTC in 1929.

Many of the UTC issues were suitably endorsed reprints of items that had previously been released in the UK. The set RIDERS OF THE WORLD issued in 1931 proved to be a very durable set, as it had first been issued in the UK by John Player in 1905. There were also series illustrating South Africa's birds, butterflies and wild flowers, and the national sport of rugby union was not overlooked. The set of SOUTH AFRICAN RUGBY FOOTBALL CLUBS issued in 1933 is a typical example. Another associate of BAT, Westminster Tobacco, was also actively issuing cards between the wars as was Gallaher from 1934, as a result of acquiring the export businesses of International Tobacco and Peter Jackson. Related to these latter companies was the firm of A & M Wix who issued some lengthy series between 1935 and 1940 with Max cigarettes. The 500 cards in their CINEMA CAVALCADE and the three series of FILM FAVOURITES, each of 100 cards, provide a marvellous record of the pre-1940 cinema.

Taddy **Admirals & Generals – the War** (Cape Town back), c1914 (F, per card)

A & M Wix **Film Favourites 3rd Series**, 1939 (I, set of 100)

United Tobacco Companies **South African Rugby Football Clubs**, c1933 (G, set of 65 large)

EUROPE

In 1902 when the agreement establishing BAT was entered into, Ireland was considered part of the British market. There was, therefore, no question of it forming part of BAT's sales territory. With the establishment of the Irish Free State in 1922 the situation changed and the country became an export market for British manufacturers. In 1923 the Wills branch set up a manufacturing facility in Dublin and was quickly followed by John Player. Wills issued a number of series aimed at their Irish customers,

for example IRISH HOLIDAY RESORTS, IRISH INDUSTRIES, SHANNON ELECTRIC POWER SCHEME and IRISH SPORTSMEN. Player generally relied on the sets issued in the home market but did reprint some old series, such as WONDERS OF THE WORLD and WRESTLING & JU-JITSU, with different coloured backs. With the advent of adhesive cards the Irish sets can be distinguished as the 'album clause' omits the price.

Other British firms were also marketing their cigarettes in Ireland and providing stiff competition for the local firms. T P & R

Player **Wonders of the World** (grey back), 1926 (F, set of 25)

Goodbody, who had issued a number of series up to 1916, ceded control to Cope Bros in 1924 but the business was later closed down and the goodwill passed to another Irish firm, P J Carroll & Co. Whilst Ireland was considered a home market, the Channel Islands were not, and the familiar pattern of BAT using ITC brands was repeated. John Player seem to have been the most popular with BIRDS & THEIR YOUNG, NATIONAL FLAGS AND ARMS and RAF BADGES among the sets issued, without the ITC Clause, of course. The Guernsey firm of Bucktrout

became associated with BAT and issued a few sets in the 1920s and Ching & Co is one of the rare tobacco companies to have produced cards since 1940.

In terms of quantity of cards the Germans must rank a close second to the UK tobacco houses. Although German manufacturers only warmed to the idea after the 1914/18 war, they were soon producing sets which commonly exceeded 200 cards. With the rise to power of Hitler and the National Socialist Party the subject matter became increasingly propagandist. An

Brinkmann
Das Waffenstarrende Ausland, c1935
(G, set of 300 mixed sizes)

Greiling **Greiling–Munz-Sammlung**, c1930 (A, per card)

Ver. Staaten, 10 Dollars, Vorderseite (Gold) = 42,00 RM

Tiedemanns **Norges Dyreliv I Sjoen**, c1935 (A, per card)

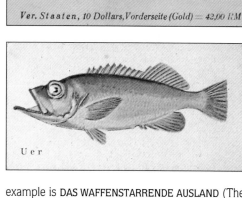
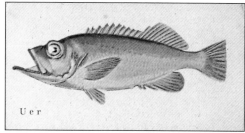

Uer

Cousis **Actors and Actresses***, (framework back) c1905 (A, per card)

example is DAS WAFFENSTARRENDE AUSLAND (The Armed Forces of Other Countries) from Brinkmann which consists of 200 small and 100 large cards. The intention of this series was, no doubt, to remind the population that as others were well-armed, Germany needed to be too. There are, however, many extremely attractive series ranging from buildings, costumes and works of art to motoring, aviation, film stars and sport. As seen above, sets sometimes consist of two different sizes of card and are often made up in sections.

A fairly typical series is DIE BUNTE WELT (The Coloured World), issued by both Jasmatzi and Salem, which pictures people, animals and artefacts from around the globe. One of the most attractive series, running to 641 cards, was produced by Greiling and features the world's coinage. The coins are nicely embossed in realistic colours against a white background. The problem of collecting such long series was solved by the manufacturers inserting coupons in the packets exchangeable for specific groups of cards. This avoided the frustration of never knowing when a set would be completed but also meant the excitement of the chase was lost. Another feature of the German system was the sale of very handsome albums in which collectors could house their cards.

France, Spain, Italy and the Benelux countries appear to have produced very few cards, although BAT did release some series in Belgium with their Albert and Copain brands. The Turkish-Macedonian Tobacco Co also circulated a few Dutch language cards and silks. Scandinavia yields a better reward although none of the cards issued there are easy to come by. Five of Cope's series can be collected with printing in the Danish language and Teofani distributed a set of 50 large cards of ICELANDIC EMPLOYEES* from their base in Reykjavic. Norwegian cards can be found issued by H Petteroe, an associate of BAT, P A Larsen, who number among their series a set similar to Player's 'BONZO' DOGS and J L Tiedemanns. This latter firm issued a lengthy SPORTS SERIES* and, appropriately, a set of 12 featuring Norwegian fish and sea life.

Malta is a country which has a surprisingly rich tradition of card issues. Possibly the large British Naval Base was an important factor. BAT, through their associated company Westminster Tobacco, had a good share of the market and the Wills and Player brands were also popular. BEAUTIES–BROWN TINTED* is thought to have been issued on the Island during the 1910/1915 period and Player's series of 25 DOGS FROM PAINTINGS BY ARTHUR WARDLE was distributed there in 1927. Local manufacturers also had active card-issuing programmes and one of the most prolific was Cousis & Co. Most of their output was photographic and dates from between 1900 to 1918. Many extremely lengthy series of actresses, celebrities, views and warships were produced by this firm. Colombos was also distributing cards at much the same time among which were five photographic series of FAMOUS OIL PAINTINGS. They also issued a series on the LIFE OF NAPOLEON BONAPARTE and complemented this with similar productions honouring Nelson and Wellington.

In the 1920s both the Atlam Cigarette Factory and Camler Tobacco issued cards – the former producing VIEWS OF MALTA*, VIEWS OF THE WORLD* and no less than 519 CELEBRITIES*. Camler's output was restricted to footballers and a series of MALTESE FAMILIES COATS OF ARMS. The local firm most active during the inter-war period was John Scerri. Several sets were produced, including BEAUTIES AND CHILDREN*, CINEMA STARS, FILM STARS, INTERESTING PLACES OF THE WORLD and MEMBERS OF PARLIAMENT–MALTA.

BRITISH-AMERICAN TOBACCO CO LTD (BAT)

This company was registered on 29 September 1902 with an authorised capital of £6 million. It was originally wholly owned by the ITC and the ATC and took over from them their export businesses, including brands, agencies and licences. In 1912 BAT became a quoted company on the London Stock Exchange, following the break up of the ATC. At that time its market capitalisation was £31 million. It was not until 1979, however, that the ITC disposed of its substantial shareholding in BAT.

The fact that BAT acquired the brands and trademarks of its parent organisations for all export markets can be confusing. For example, as from 1902 the purchaser of Player's Navy Cut cigarettes in the Channel Islands, or a buyer of Wills' Three Castles brand in Australia, were acquiring BAT products. And any cards inserted in those packs were BAT issues even though the Player and Wills name might be shown on the reverse.

The same situation applied to the ATC brands such as, Cameo marketed in Australia and Pinhead in China. The rule is that when no accreditation is given on the card to the ITC or the ATC, then it is a BAT issue. There are a few instances, particularly in the 1902/1905 period, when BAT's own name appeared on the cards. BEAUTIES – WATER GIRLS* is a typical example of this early period.

BAT's marketing skills were such that there were very few countries where they did not sell cigarettes at one time or another. For language or logistical reasons cards were often printed without brand details or with completely plain backs. There is thus no obvious way of knowing the country of origin for these items. Many of the sets so issued mirrored the ITC domestic card printings. For example, Ogden's BOY SCOUTS 1929 domestic issue was used by BAT without any reference to Ogden's or BAT on the reverse. Churchman's RAILWAY WORKING home issue in two series of 25, was reprinted as a set of 50 for John Player and inserted with cigarettes sold in New Zealand. The same set of 50 was also produced for BAT with the Wills name on the back and further printed without any mention of the Player or Wills names. BAT's records show that this latter set was intended for use in Malaya.

Player's HINTS ON ASSOCIATION FOOTBALL was an interesting case where, for the reprint, the features of the footballers were altered to make them look oriental. The issue was intended for the Far Eastern market but customers cannot have been too impressed, as large numbers of the cards were remaindered. This does mean, however, that collectors today can purchase the set very cheaply. Although a large proportion of BAT's cards were first issued by other manufacturers, there are some original items to be collected. This is particularly the case for cinema stars and modern beauties of which several series were produced.

Today, British-American Tobacco is part of BAT Industries plc, a huge international group with operations in more than 80 countries.

BAT **Beauties – Water Girls***, c1903 (B, per card)

BAT **Hints on Association Football***, c1934 (C, set of 48)

105

BAA, BAA, BLACK SHEEP.

WOOL BAG

FRY'S COCOA & CHOCOLATE
MAKERS TO H.M. THE KING.

LITTLE MISS MUFFET

FRY'S COCOA & CHOCOLATE
MAKERS TO H.M. THE KING.

THERE WAS AN OLD WOMAN TOSSED UP IN A BASKET

FRY'S COCOA & CHOCOLATE
MAKERS TO H.M. THE KING.

MARY MARY QUITE CONTRARY.

FRY'S COCOA & CHOCOLATE
MAKERS TO H.M. THE KING.

Jim Armfield

Ron Springett

Jimmy Greaves

Maurice Setters

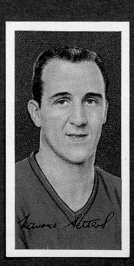

CHAPTER 8

TRADE CARDS

Cigarette cards are, of course, trade cards but this chapter covers those organisations, other than tobacco companies, who issued picture cards as a means of promoting their products. Cards that were produced with the intention that customers and clients might collect them, date back to the 1860s or even earlier. The fact that the commercial applications of chromolithography were developed at the same time is no coincidence. Prior to this, the tradesman's card was generally printed in black with name, address, brief details of the trade and, possibly, a pictorial symbol representing the nature of the trade. These cards would have been used in a similar way to today's business visiting cards and compliment slips.

The first user of picture cards on any meaningful scale was the proprietor of the *Au Bon Marché* store in Paris, Jacques-Aristide Boucicaut. Originally a partner, Boucicaut took over sole responsibility for the shop in 1863 and, with his wife and son, developed a relatively small establishment into the largest dry goods business in the world. It has been estimated that over 400 series of cards were issued by the firm, all superbly printed by chromolithography and often featuring well-dressed ladies or young children. The cards were issued in series of six or more, usually in fairly large sizes and most were carefully arranged and pasted into albums by their proud owners. That is why it is hard to find these cards today without some damage to the backs.

The idea of issuing cards to reward and retain customers was quickly copied by others. Printing firms were soon preparing stock designs and it is not too unusual to find the same picture issued by more than one business house. And it was not just the grocery stores who used cards, as we can find them printed with the names of ladies' and gentlemens' outfitters, music shops, toy shops, manufacturers of pills and potions, blenders of coffee and tea and purveyors of sweets and chocolates. Among the latter were the firms of Chocolat Payraud, Guerin-Boutron of Paris, Cacao Bensdorp of Amsterdam and Maestrani of Switzerland.

LIEBIG

In mainland Europe especially, cards printed in colour are usually referred to as 'chromos', and the company that made its name synonymous with chromos was a manufacturer of an unlikely product – meat extract. In fact, in the middle of the 19th century the time was ripe for a cheap and nutritious food that was hygienically packed and easily transportable. The man who perfected the process was a German chemist called Justus von Liebig, who published his treatise on the subject in 1847. In the 1860s the first South American processing plant was constructed at Fray Bentos in Uruguay, where a huge cattle ranch was also established. The initial card series from the Liebig Company was issued in 1872 as a set of twelve and featured the factory premises at Fray Bentos. The following year von Liebig died but the card programme was to continue for another one hundred years with breaks only during the two world wars. In all, 1,863 different series were

Au Bon Marché **Boy and Girl in Country Scenes***, c1880 (A, per extra large card) (size 123 x 82mm)

page 106, left to right
First row:
Fry **Nursery Rhymes**, 1917 (J, set of 50)

Second and third rows:
Brooke Bond **British Birds**, 1954 (E, set of 20)

Fourth row:
Barratt **Famous Footballers A9**, 1961 (H, set of 50)

Liebig (F 726) **Chasing the Butterfly**, 1903
(G, set of 6 extra large)
(size 82 x 110mm)

issued, the vast majority being in unnumbered sets of six. The size was usually a little smaller than a normal postcard and frequently cards were issued in more than one language. To collect every card in every language would result in a total of around 5,000 sets. Up to 1914 the cards were issued freely to customers but subsequently sets were exchanged against coupons printed on the packaging of the product.

An enormous range of subjects was covered including animals and architecture, birds and butterflies, children and costumes, fishes and folklore, scientists, sculptors, travel and typewriters. The backs were sometimes decorated with attractive line drawings and a few sets issued in the early 1900s actually illustrated the cattle ranching operations in Uruguay. One drawback to these cards, beautiful as most of them are, is that the text is rarely

Liebig (F 231) **British Army Uniforms**, 1889
(F, per extra large card)

printed in English. For some reason very few cards were issued in Britain and, when found, they are expensive. But despite the problems of the language, the pictures are so interesting that every collection should have at least a few sets.

Fortunately, Liebig was very conscious of their collecting public and kept records of the various card sets issued. This has enabled catalogues to be produced of which the most comprehensive are those published by Fada and Sanguinetti. The success of Liebig's product spawned several imitators and cards from these rival firms do surface from time to time. Perhaps the best are those produced by Cibils. To help counter this competition, each card Liebig issued had depicted on the front a pot or tube of the 'genuine' product and on the reverse appeared the signature 'J v Liebig' in blue lettering.

Prior to 1905 British issuers of trade cards were pretty thin on the ground, although some very charming sets were issued by biscuit

makers Huntley & Palmer. Here again though, some of these were for issue on the Continent and are in the French language. Thomas Holloway, the pharmaceutical firm, issued a few series and the businesses of Kardomah and Lever Brothers put out large numbers of cards but mostly in black and white. For English language cards in the Continental style we have, in fact, to travel to North America.

NORTH AMERICA

All kinds of firms sponsored card issues, from local hardware stores to international manufacturers. Many of the early cards issued in the United States were printed in Germany or France and those that were produced locally during the 1870s and '80s were generally of inferior quality.

Among many attractive cards, those produced by J & P Coats, the thread manufacturers, and the sewing machine companies such as Singer, Wheeler & Wilson, Household and Domestic, can sometimes be found tucked away in dealers' stockbooks. Often the backs of these cards are plain, but those with descriptions of the product

Lever Bros **Celebrities***,
c1902 (B, per large card)

Babbitt **Advertisement Card***, c1895
(B, per extra large card)

Church & Dwight **Useful Birds of America, Ninth Series**, c1940
(C, set of 12 medium)

Red-breasted Grosbeak

being sold, or other advertising messages, do have added interest. The New York firm of B T Babbitt printed this splendid message on the back of one of their trade cards:

'Many of us become unhappy on account of our inability to carry out our chosen plans or to help our friends when in need. You can't always gratify your benevolent impulses by lending one hundred dollars, or relieving the pressing wants of those whose condition demands help, but you can always do a friend a good turn by recommending him always to use B T BABBITT'S MEDICINAL YEAST, this being the strongest and purest in the world.'

By the 1890s a number of companies were issuing cards in series and among those that are easiest to find are items from Arbuckle Coffee Co and Church & Dwight. The latter firm were manufacturers of baking soda and produced a stream of lovely cards right through and beyond World War I. They concentrated on the natural world with special emphasis on birds and the 9th and 10th series of USEFUL BIRDS OF AMERICA are currently catalogued at less than £10.00 per set.

BRITISH TRADE CARDS

By 1905 the number of British trade firms issuing cards had started to grow. Well to the fore were the confectionery manufacturers with cards being distributed by Barratt & Co, Cadbury, J S Fry & Sons, James Keiller, John Mackintosh, Maynards, James Pascall and Rowntree. BRITISH COLONIES, MAPS AND INDUSTRIES* was issued by Cadbury around 1908 and the fifth of the six cards illustrates the island of Trinidad. Also pictured are some local workers picking the cocoa beans on Cadbury's own plantation. The well known Dairy Milk Tray and Bournville Cocoa brands were launched in 1905 and 1906 respectively and Cadbury's FLAG SERIES advertises both on the reverse of the cards. The colourful SHIPPING SERIES from about 1910 was printed in four different large sizes and the wording on the back states 'Specially made and packed for export'.

The Bristol firm of J S Fry was established in 1728 and produced many fine series. Among the first were two sets of 25 cards called DAYS OF NELSON and DAYS OF WELLINGTON. Included in the latter is a picture of the exclusive Waterloo Medal, which was issued only to officers and other ranks who fought at the Battle of Waterloo. Another of Britain's heroes, the polar explorer Robert Scott, was rewarded with an individual series titled WITH CAPTAIN SCOTT AT THE SOUTH POLE. Among the early issues from Pascall was a BOY SCOUT SERIES*, this being a popular subject following the founding of the movement in 1908. Much less common are cards featuring Lord Baden-Powell's sister organisation, so Maynards' GIRL GUIDE SERIES* has a scarcity value from this factor alone.

Dating early cards is normally difficult so it is a bonus to find cards which are dated. One such is Walker Harrison and Garthwaites' fine series of DOGS* which has the calendar for 1902 on the reverse. This was an appropriate subject for a dog biscuit manufacturer but packing the cards must have been a problem. Even more of a mystery is how Nugget Polish managed to insert their superb ALLIED SERIES in tins of boot polish without the large sized cards getting contaminated. Many firms produced 'war series' during the 1914/18 conflict, including Home

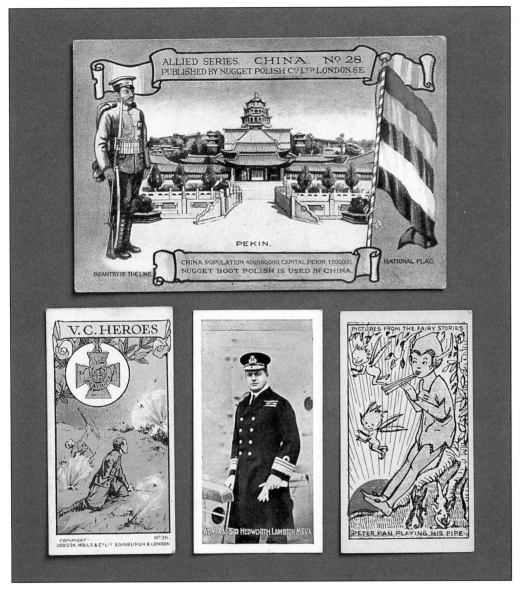

Maynards **Girl Guide Series***, c1920 (D, per card)

and Colonial Stores, Maypole and Meadow Dairy. The Edinburgh firm of Alex Ferguson put out a fine series of 41 VC HEROES and Needler issued a MILITARY SERIES* with their Military Mints.

The period between the wars was not marked by a huge increase in trade cards. The confectionery companies were still active, with Cadbury's TRANSPORT, and ANCIENT SUNDIALS from Fry, being among the more interesting. Barratt produced several series of FAMOUS FOOTBALLERS and FAMOUS CRICKETERS which have now become quite scarce. Another confectioner, the Liverpool firm of Edmondson & Co, put out a number of series including BRITISH SHIPS, FAMOUS CASTLES and PICTURES FROM THE FAIRY STORIES. Typhoo Tea packed some pleasant standard sized cards with their blends during the 1920s, including ANCIENT & ANNUAL CUSTOMS and COMMON OBJECTS HIGHLY MAGNIFIED. But towards the end of the decade they switched to an extra long card which enabled the picture and the text to appear on the front. This left the back free for special offers and advertisements which, as many of the

Top to bottom

Left row:
Fry **Days of Wellington**, 1906 (C, per card)

Middle row:
Cadbury **Flag Series**, 1912 (F, set of 12)
Cadbury **Transport**, 1925 (B, set of 25)

Right row:
Fry **With Captain Scott at the South Pole**, 1912 (C, per card)

series are multi-backed, gives extra spice to the collecting of these cards. They are certainly among the most attractive of the period.

PERIODICAL CARDS

An important offshoot of trade cards are periodical cards and a number of publishing companies started to distribute these during the 1920s. Amalgamated Press with their *Champion* and *Triumph* battled with great rivals D C Thomson, whose comics included *Rover* and *Wizard*. The *Champion* in 1922 started on a long series of SPORTSMEN* consisting of real photographs of such heroes as jockey Steve Donoghue, boxer Jack Dempsey and cricketer Jack Hobbs. *Boys' Friend* and *Boys' Magazine* were others who wooed the young readers with sportsmen, the latter putting out some peculiarly named 'ZAT CARDS which were, in fact, pictures of cricketers.

The Nelson Lee Library in 1922 tried a different subject with MODERN BRITISH LOCOMOTIVES but most publishers, including *Pals*, stuck to football. Their 1922 offering was a FOOTBALL SERIES which included a team photo of Liverpool FC. Thomson had the great idea of a double-sided card featuring a footballer on the

front and a motor car on the back. Thomson's later WIZARD SERIES contained several sub-headings such as FAMOUS LINERS, WONDERS OF THE RAIL and MOTOR CYCLES.

The schoolgirl magazines also issued cards,

Thomson **Wizard Series – Motor Cycles**, c1928 (B, per card)

---

page 113

Typhoo Tea, large cards, *left to right*

First and second cards, top row:
Characters from Shakespeare, 1937 (E, set of 25)

Third and fourth cards, top row:
Trees of the Countryside, 1937 (D, set of 25)

First and second cards, bottom row:
Wild Flowers in their Families 2nd Series, 1936 (D, set of 25)

Third and fourth cards, bottom row:
Animal Offence & Defence, c1928 (F, set of 25)

Radio Review **Broadcasting Stars***, 1935
(H, set of 20 extra large)
(size 251 x 96mm)

Barratt **Willum**, 1961
(B, per card)

POST-WAR TRENDS

After the 1939/45 war there was a cautious resumption of card issues. Barratt had continued distributing cards with sweet cigarettes throughout the war and for their first post-war series they returned to issuing FAMOUS FOOTBALLERS. This, indeed, is a theme they have continuously used right through to the 1990s. The size of the cards changed from medium to small in the mid-1950s so that when WALT DISNEY CHARACTERS* ran to two series, the first in 1955 was a larger sized card than the second, which appeared in 1957. Since the war the firm has used a much wider variety of subjects and, although a number have been TV related, there has been much else besides. WILLUM, TEST CRICKETERS and THUNDERBIRDS are sets that are now fairly scarce but HISTORICAL BUILDINGS, FISH AND BAIT and WHAT DO YOU KNOW? are among many that are relatively easy to find. Cards are still being issued today but the sponsoring company has changed its name, firstly from Barratt to Geo Bassett and then, more recently, to Trebor Bassett.

although on a much reduced scale, but the emphasis here was on cinema stars. *Radio Review* was a popular magazine of the 1930s which issued two very fine sets of BROADCASTING STARS* in 1935 and 1936. Those pictured included Ambrose, Freddie Grisewood, Tommy Handley and the Director of the BBC Dance Orchestra, Henry Hall.

At first there were a number of other firms issuing cards with sweet cigarettes, or candy sticks as they are now called, but in recent years most of them have closed or been taken over. Cards of these smaller companies are becoming

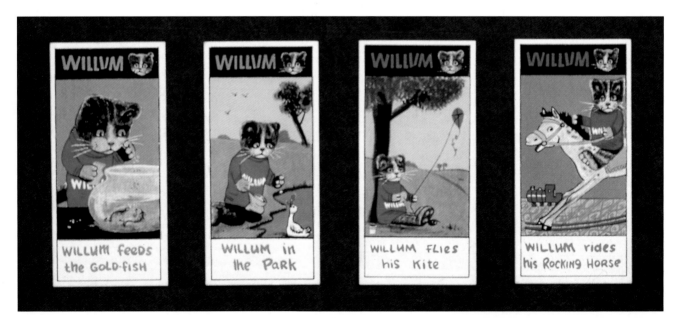

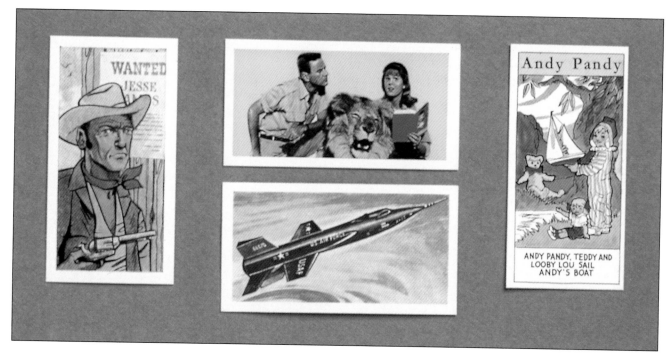

less easy to find although there are still quite a few sets available for a pound or two. Cadet, Clevedon, Como, Goodies, Kane, Primrose and Sweetule are just some of the confectionery firms that issued cards through to the 1970s. Chewing gum manufacturers were also quick to see the possibilities of picture cards. A & B C Chewing Gum were formed in 1949 and ROYAL PORTRAITS* in 1953 was their first set.

Subsequently, the subject matter became more attuned to the juvenile market with many football, pop star and TV-related series. Other firms, including Anglo-American Chewing Gum, Somportex, Monty Gum and Soccer Bubble Gum, enjoyed some success but eventually all were beaten by American competition. Even A & B C lost its independence when it became a subsidiary of Topps Chewing Gum Inc.

Typhoo Tea had been a significant issuer of cards pre-war but when they eventually restarted in the mid-1950s they concentrated mainly on pictures that had to be cut from the package. The first tea cards proper came from Barbers Teas who issued a series of 25 LOCOMOTIVES in June 1953. They followed the next year with AEROPLANES and altogether issued six series. But 1954 was to see an altogether more significant entry into the ranks of card issuing firms. On 16 August Brooke Bond started distributing a series of 20 cards of BRITISH BIRDS, which were designed by Frances Pitt. The next series of WILD FLOWERS launched in 1955 ran to 50 cards and Brooke Bond's reputation for fine wildlife and natural history cards was firmly established. The policy adopted by them, of giving credit to the artists and

Top to bottom

Left row:
Sweetule **The Wild West** (blue back), 1960 (A, set of 25)

Middle row:
Cadet **Daktari**, 1968 (B, set of 25)
Como **Speed, 1st Series**, 1962 (F, set of 25)

Right row:
Primrose **Andy Pandy**, 1960 (C, set of 50)

Opposite left

Left:
Barratt **Walt Disney Characters 2nd Series***, 1957 (I, set of 50)

Right:
Barratt **Walt Disney Characters*** (1st Series), 1955 (I, set of 35 medium)

Brooke Bond, *top to bottom*

Left row:
The Race into Space, 1971
(B, set of 50)

Middle row:
Asian Wild Life, 1962
(C, set of 50)

Right row:
Olympic Greats, 1979
(C, set of 40)

authors responsible for the card issues, has been an added bonus. Collectors owe a great debt to Brooke Bond for their sustained commitment to picture cards during the last 40 years. In 1993 an organisation called TEAMS established a club catering for Brooke Bond card enthusiasts.

Many other tea companies, including Amaran, Badshah, Browne Bros, Cooper & Co, Glengettie, Lamberts of Norwich, J Lyons, Priory and Ringtons, issued some attractive series but rarely have they reached the standard of Brooke Bond. A point to watch when collecting cards

from the smaller companies is that they frequently issued 'alike' series. For example, PEOPLE & PLACES issued by Lamberts was also distributed by seven other companies including Barratt. Brooke Bond branches abroad also issued cards and some of these, especially those distributed in the USA, are very hard to collect.

The packaging of breakfast cereals, like tea, lends itself to the issuing of cards. Kellogg put out a series of 40 MOTOR CARS* in 1950 but then used package designs before returning to cards in 1962. They then issued a number of

HEARTS OF OAK Drybrook

THE RAILWAY
Gillingham

THE BIRD IN HAND Bridgwater

fine series such as SHIPS OF THE BRITISH NAVY and VETERAN MOTOR CARS. Morning Foods was another whose first issues came out in the early '50s with BRITISH PLANES and TEST CRICKETERS. Among the other cereal companies that have used cards are Quaker Oats, Weetabix and Nabisco. Ice lollies and ice cream would not appear to be ideal products when it comes to distributing cards but Mister Softee, Lyons Maid, Wall's and Rossi have succeeded extremely well. The latter's two series of THE HISTORY OF FLIGHT are well worth collecting.

Packaging is, in fact, rarely a problem, as such diverse commodities as petrol, hair grips, milk products, fish, potato crisps, cooking fat, stockings, whisky and beer have all successfully used cards as a promotional aid. Whitbread's many series of INN SIGNS were extremely well produced and are eagerly collected today. So are the cards issued by ABC Cinemas and the various sporting portraits put out by *The Daily Herald* and *News Chronicle* in the 1950s. A more modern phenomenon has been the many series of cards issued by a number of the regional police forces. The fact that the underlying message is important does not make the cards any less fun to collect.

Trade cards have been, and still are, issued worldwide. The Liebig cards mentioned earlier were produced up until 1973 and cards from the continental chocolate firms of Suchard, Van Houten, Stollwerck and Tobler do turn up in this country. The Italian coffee firm of Lavazza issued 272 series of cards in the 1950s and 1960s, all in sets of six and similar in size to the Liebig issues. Australia and New Zealand are also fruitful sources of trade cards. The Sanitarium Health Food Co has been a regular producer of cards since 1946, many in large and extra large sizes. Anyone who has managed to collect even half of these cards will have acquired a colourful and informative library. For sports enthusiasts cards to look for include those from A W Allen and Australian Licorice in the pre-1939 period and from Australian Dairy and Scanlen's Gum in more recent years.

Whitbread, medium sized cards

Left to right:
Inn Signs, Maritime, 1974
(C, set of 25)
The Railway, 1958
(B, single card issue)
Inn Signs, Devon & Somerset, 1973
(G, set of 25)

Sanitarium **'Our Golden Fleece'**, 1981
(B, set of 20 large)

Great Dane

PLAYER'S CIGARETTES

HOUND

Pascall SWEETS and CHOCOLATES

Hignett's Cigarettes

West Highland White Terrier

WELSH CORGI

ENGLISH SETTER PUPPIES

FLAT-COATED RETRIEVER

PLAYER'S CIGARETTES.

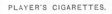
KING CHARLES SPANIEL.

POINTER

OGDEN'S CIGARETTES.

"HOT POT."

CHAPTER 9

THEMATIC COLLECTING

Specialisation, or collecting on a thematic basis, is the most common method of collecting cards today. Even people with large general collections usually come to a stage where, in order to find additional stimulation, they set aside part of their collection to a subject of special interest.

Many, of course, are drawn into card collecting in the first place by another hobby or pastime, or perhaps because of their job. Thus soccer fans collect football cards, golfers are attracted to golf cards, ornithologists find bird cards of special interest, policemen might look for cards depicting the police force, and so on.

Like any other method of collecting, subject or thematic collecting needs thought and planning. The range of cards is so great and the opportunities for diversification so large, that it is best to outline in your mind or, better still, on paper, the parameters of your proposed thematic collection.

For example, the football enthusiast has the choice of trying to locate every card on the subject ever issued, or just collecting items featuring one particular player. Even if the ultimate aim is to collect every single card it is best to start in a modest fashion and concentrate on just cigarette cards or trade cards. With a subject such as football, which issuing companies have found so popular, it would probably take the best part of a lifetime to track down all the cards issued by any one of such companies as Taddy, Godfrey Phillips or Barratt/Bassett.

Sporting cards have attracted a number of devotees over the years who have painstakingly compiled comprehensive lists. So if your collecting theme is going to be football, cricket, golf, boxing or tennis, then you can get off to a flying start by buying the appropriate reference book. If your interests lie elsewhere, be prepared to do some research work of your own. To many, this is the most interesting part of thematic collecting.

Those who wish to form a collection on, say, aircraft, dogs, motor cars or natural history, can generally find much of what they need to know by careful study of the *World and Trade Indexes* and the catalogues published by the major dealers. In this chapter the aim is to break down

Underrated in the past, football cards are now sought after

Left:
Carreras **Footballers***, 1934 (H, set of 75)

Right:
Player **Footballers, Caricatures by 'Rip'**, 1926 (G, set of 50)

Dogs, a popular choice as a collecting theme, *top to bottom*

Left row:
Ogden's Tabs (BAT) **Animals*** (with caption), 1913 (J, set of 60)
Barratt **Animals in the Service of Man**, 1964 (A, set of 25)
Gallaher **Dogs** (1st Series),1936 (E, set of 48)
Player **Dogs** (heads, 1st Series), 1927 (G, set of 25)

Middle row:
Player **Boy Scout & Girl Guide Patrol Signs**, 1933 (D, set of 50)
Pattreiouex **Dogs**, 1939 (D, set of 48 medium)
Gallaher **Dogs**, (caption in block) 1934 (D, set of 24 large)

Right row:
Pascall **Dogs***, 1924 (G, set of 18)
Hignett **Dogs**, 1936 (H, set of 50)
Gallaher **Dogs Second Series**, 1938 (E, set of 48)
Ogden's **Greyhound Racing 2nd Series**, 1928 (H, set of 25)

Cards on golf, aviation, motor cars and cricket are always in demand

Top to bottom

Left row:
Ogden's **Champions of 1936**, 1937 (H, set of 50)

Middle row:
Player **International Air Liners**, 1936 (D, set of 50)
Priory Tea **Cars**, 1964 (D, set of 50)

Right row:
Ardath **Cricket, Tennis & Golf Celebrities**, 1935 (G, set of 50)

Opposite

Fire-fighting is a less common theme

Right: Player **Fire-Fighting Appliances**, 1930 (H, set of 50)
Left: Ogden's **Air-Raid Precautions**, 1938 (F, set of 50)

some of broad categories and look at a few interesting sidelines that could be the basis for a thematic collection.

HOW TO START

The first place to start is with you – the collector. Look at where you live, your job, your leisure time pursuits, your last holiday or even the subjects that fascinated you at school. If you live in a large town or city then it is quite feasible to put together a collection of cards relating to your home town. If you reside in a small town or village then your 'county' could be the basis for a thematic collection.

Holidays and travel also provide enormous scope. If your skills include making special displays then you can augment your photographs and other holiday ephemera with cards depicting places visited, mode of transport and the people, buildings and historical events associated with the location. Most occupations provide the basis for a theme, whether the job be agricultural worker or zoo-keeper. A railway employee would have to be selective to keep the collection within reasonable bounds, as would a member of the armed forces. The bank clerk or

plumber may have more difficulty in building up a sizeable collection but the cards are there to be found.

Nostalgia and a desire to find out more about our background, is often a powerful stimulus. Childhood events and memories can transform a collection into a biographical statement. Your father's or mother's job, the first pet, a holiday

by the seaside, travelling on a tram, learning to swim, joining the Boy Scouts or Girl Guides, a visit to London, wartime or national service, the first car or motorcycle, favourite radio or television programmes, a visit to the theatre or cinema – the memorable things in our lives can usually be recalled with the help of cards.

When we turn to leisure interests it really is a case of 'the sky's the limit!' Even if social activities are confined mainly to the pub and the television, there is no need to despair. There are many attractive cartophilic 'pub-crawls' that can be found and a whole host of popular television programmes have been recorded on cards. Most sports are well covered as are the various methods of transport. Antique collectors, balloonists, campers, do-it-yourself enthusiasts, Egyptologists, fortune-tellers, gardeners, all the way alphabetically to yachtsmen and zoogeographers, can build up a theme to enhance their hobby.

A COUNTY COLLECTION

One of the more popular themes is the formation of a county collection. Individual collectors would, no doubt, choose the county of their birth or the region in which they currently reside, but for purely illustrative purposes let us look at the county of Warwickshire. Situated in the heart of the British Isles, it has many fine traditions, much beautiful scenery and several important industries.

Topography and architecture

A good place to start is with topographical series such as Hill's VIEWS OF INTEREST and Pattreiouex's photographical sets from the late 1930s. Hill immediately rewards us in the first of their five series with an attractive tinted photograph of the Shakespeare Memorial Theatre at Stratford. Warwick Castle is also pictured in its commanding position over the River Avon and other cards feature Kenilworth Castle and Birmingham Council House. Royal Leamington Spa, itself the subject of a set of cards in 1971, is featured in VIEWS OF INTEREST THIRD SERIES and Rugby School, founded in 1567, appears in the FOURTH SERIES.

Not surprisingly, Wills also feature Rugby in

their series of 25 PUBLIC SCHOOLS. The artist has depicted a portion of the famous School Close with some boys enjoying a game of cricket. The school is, however, much more famous for the origination of the game of rugby football and for the novel *Tom Brown's Schooldays*. Former pupils from the school, including rugby players, provide additional scope for the theme. One old boy was former Prime Minister, Neville Chamberlain. He can be seen in NOTABLE MPS put out by Carreras in 1929. Wills have many other helpful series including a handsome set of BEAUTIFUL HOMES. Compton Wynyates, a home of the Marquess of Northampton, is shown on card no.10 and the imposing Stoneleigh Abbey graces card no.24. The extensive series of BOROUGH ARMS* put out by the same firm features Warwick and Stratford-upon-Avon on cards 77 and 124 respectively.

Pattreiouex were renowned for their medium sized real photographic cards issued with Senior Service cigarettes in the years immediately preceding World War II. Several cards cover Warwick and Stratford, including delightful studies of Shakespeare's birthplace and Anne Hathaway's cottage from SIGHTS OF BRITAIN. A short distance along the A439 is Bidford Bridge and just a few miles from there is the equally charming Wixford Bridge. Both appear in Pattreiouex's THE BRIDGES OF BRITAIN.

Close by is the tiny village of Marlcliff, which has the deserved distinction of being one of Ogden's 50 PICTURESQUE VILLAGES. The same issuer put out an excellent series in 1932 called BY THE ROADSIDE and here we can find Harvard House at Stratford-upon-Avon and The Old Cross at Meriden. This cross is traditionally considered to be the exact centre of England. The card informs us that nearby is a War Memorial erected to honour cyclists who died in the Great War. Another Ogden's issue, BROADCASTING, pictures Studio 2 in Birmingham, which is stated on the card to be the head-quarters of the Midland Region of the BBC. The set titled INTERESTING SIDELIGHTS ON THE WORK OF THE GPO may not seem a promising place to look, but Lambert & Butler included in it a picture and details of Rugby Radio Station on card no.47.

Neville Chamberlain, Rugby scholar and Mayor of Birmingham
Carreras **Notable MPs**, 1929 (F, set of 50)

page 122
Some of Warwickshire's architectural features
Left to right:
Hill, *first row*:
Views of Interest First Series, 1938
(C, set of 48 large)

Typhoo Tea, *second row*:
Homes of Famous Men, 1934 (D, set of 25 large)

Pattreiouex, *third row*:
Sights of Britain, (1st Series), 1936
(C, set of 48 medium)
The Bridges of Britain, 1938 (C, set of 48 medium)

Wills, *fourth row*:
Beautiful Homes, 1930 (G, set of 25 large)
Public Schools, 1927 (H, set of 25 large)

KENILWORTH CASTLE

VICTORIA SQUARE, BIRMINGHAM

"Homes of Famous Men'
SHAKESPEARE'S BIRTHPLACE,
STRATFORD-ON-AVON
England's greatest poet and
dramatist! This is one of the
most famous and best-known
birthplaces in the world—indeed, it is referred to simply
as The "Birthplace." This little
house at Stratford probably at-
tracts more visitors than any
other in the country. Bought for
the nation in 1847, it was carefully restored ten years later
*Portrait by courtesy of The National
Portrait Gallery.*
Ty.phoo Series of 25   No. 18

William Shakspeare

ANN HATHAWAY'S COTTAGE

WIXFORD BRIDGE, WARWICKSHIRE

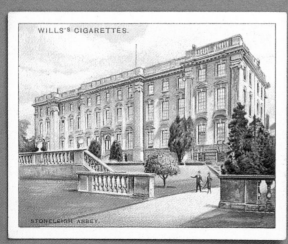

WILLS'S CIGARETTES.

STONELEIGH ABBEY.

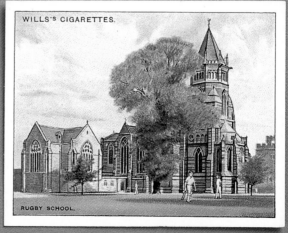

WILLS'S CIGARETTES.

RUGBY SCHOOL.

Before we go further let us return to the country houses in the area and to Player's COUNTRY SEATS AND ARMS*. With 150 cards in three series there is some overlap with the sets mentioned previously. But there are additional items including Guy's Cliffe, the seat of Earl Percy, and Compton Verney, home of Lord Willoughby de Broke. Player also devoted an entire set of 25 cards to Warwickshire's most famous son with their SHAKESPEAREAN SERIES. Tom Brown, Rugby's well-known schoolboy hero, can be found in Player's CHARACTERS FROM FICTION on card no. 23.

Sport

When it comes to sport, Warwickshire has an enviable reputation. Whilst golf would not spring immediately to mind, the Little Aston Golf Club is included amongst John Player's series of CHAMPIONSHIP GOLF COURSES. Turn to cricket or football, however, and there is an enormous amount of material available. The County Cricket Club, which celebrated its centenary in 1982, has won several major trophies. Both Churchman in their FAMOUS CRICKET COLOURS

and Kane Products in their series of CRICKET CLUBS & BADGES picture the county cap and emblem. Players who have represented the county appear in all the main cricketer series, including H W Bainbridge from Wills' CRICKETERS, 1896*, who was captain of the club

Player **Characters from Fiction**, 1933 (G, set of 25 Large)

Warwickshire, traditional and modern

Top to bottom

Ogden's, *left row*:
By the Roadside, 1932 (G, set of 50)

Ogden's, *middle row*:
Picturesque Villages, 1936 (G, set of 50)
Broadcasting, 1935 (G, set of 50)

Lambert & Butler, *right row*:
Interesting Sidelights on the Work of the GPO, 1939 (G, set of 50)

Some of Warwickshire's sporting and military connections

Left to right, top row:
Wills **Cricketers, 1896***, 1896 (G, per card)
Player **Championship Golf Courses**, 1936 (K, set of 25 large)
Churchman **Famous Cricket Colours**, 1928 (H, set of 25)

Bottom row:
Player **Association Cup Winners**, 1930 (H, set of 50)
(second & third cards) Ogden's **AFC Nicknames**, 1933 (J, set of 50)
Lingford **British War Leaders**, 1950 (G, set of 36)

when it achieved first class status.

Aston Villa and Birmingham are two of the county's famous soccer teams pictured in Ogden's colourful AFC NICKNAMES. Aston Villa have won the FA Cup many times since their first success in 1887. That winning combination is pictured in a series of 50 ASSOCIATION CUP WINNERS from John Player. An action picture of an Aston Villa v Sunderland League Match can be seen on card no.5 of Gallaher's series of 100 FOOTBALLERS.

Military and engineering

Turning to the county's military connections, the Royal Warwickshire Regiment is included in Player's REGIMENTAL COLOURS AND CAP BADGES*. Field Marshal Viscount Montgomery served in this regiment during the Great War and he is pictured in BRITISH WAR LEADERS, an excellent trade set from Lingford. Jack Payne was as well-known before the last war as Monty became during it. This popular band leader and show-man, born at Leamington Spa, is included in Lambert & Butler's DANCE BAND LEADERS.

Another fruitful sideline to explore is the county's famed engineering industry. All the famous car and motorcycle factories could form a theme of their own. Two of the prestigious marques that originated in Coventry are Riley and Alvis and examples can be seen in Brooke Bond's HISTORY OF THE MOTOR CAR.

It would be easy to go on, but hopefully the above will give a good introduction to the enjoyment that can be obtained in putting together a county collection.

CARTOPHILY AND PHILATELY

Another possibility for a thematic collection is to combine two separate hobbies. There are probably few people who have not collected stamps at some time or another. Indeed, many of the distinguished cartophilists who put card collecting on the map were former philatelists. There are many cards that feature stamps and the postal system, some easy to discover and some tucked away in unlikely places.

The set that most readily springs to mind is STAMPS RARE & INTERESTING put out by Ardath. This colourful series does not just illustrate many fabulous philatelic rarities, in many cases it also gives an interesting pictorial background relating to the stamp. By way of example, on card no.11 the drama of the first transatlantic Air Post is depicted, as Harry Hawker is rescued after crashing into the sea. There is an interesting story relating to the unremarkable

Brooke Bond **History of the Motor Car**, 1968 (B, set of 50)

The band leader Jack Payne. Lambert & Butler **Dance Band Leaders**, 1936 (I, set of 25)

Historical philatelic personalities and events

Left to right

First and last cards: Ogden's **Royal Mail**, 1909 (K, set of 50)

Middle cards: Ardath **Stamps Rare & Interesting**, 1939 (G, set of 50)

Ogden's **Royal Mail**, 1909
(K, set of 50)

Woods **Romance of the Royal Mail**, c1930
(F, set of 25)

5 centavos stamp shown on card no.34. In 1901 both Nigaragua and Panama were vying to provide the passage that would link the Atlantic and Pacific Oceans. The Nicaraguan stamp showing evidence of volcanic activity was sent to each member of the US Senate. This is thought to have been the deciding factor in turning the vote in favour of Panama.

The Royal Mail

Another series with much philatelic interest is ROYAL MAIL, issued firstly by Ogden's in 1909, and subsequently by Wm Clarke. Although scarce, the cards are well worth searching for as they cover the story of the mail in some depth. Sir Rowland Hill, as the instigator of uniform penny postage is pictured, as is an earlier reformer, Ralph Allen. The original General Post Office was in Lombard Street and is shown on card no.5 with its successor building in St Martin Le Grand illustrated on card no.50. Compare also the frenzied activity of the London City Postmen on card no.49, with the more leisurely mail delivery in rural India – by elephant!

W H & J Woods produced a set of 25 cards

on a similar theme in the early 1930s with their ROMANCE OF THE ROYAL MAIL. The introduction of the first British postcard is seen on card no.15 and the next card in the series shows a charming early mail van. Tongan 'tin can' mail is vividly portrayed, as is delivery of mail in a snowstorm on card no.25.

Moving into the post-war era, the confectionery company Sweetule Products produced a STAMP CARDS series around 1960 and Twinings Tea went one better with two different sets of 30 cards. The first of these starts with the British Guiana one cent of 1856 and also featured is the Blue Mauritius two pence of 1847. In the second series we can find an example of the interesting Brazilian 'Bulls Eye' stamp and the rare one shilling Government Parcels inverted overprint. Both series were compiled by the philatelists, L N & M Williams.

In 1983 the South Wales Constabulary distributed 36 large cards featuring British stamps, as part of their crime prevention campaign, and this initiative was followed up by the Hertfordshire, Kent and other Forces. These attractive cards are well worth looking out for.

Many cards can be found depicting postage stamps

Top to bottom, left row:
Sweetule **Stamp Cards**, 1960 (B, set of 25)

Middle row:
South Wales Constabulary **British Stamps**, 1983 (C, set of 36 extra large)
Sweetule **Stamp Cards**, 1960 (B, set of 25)

Right row:
Twinings **Rare Stamps**, (1st Series), 1958 (E, set of 30)
Twinings **Rare Stamps 2nd Series**, 1960 (B, set of 30)

Real postage stamps

It is even possible to collect real stamps on cards. The most prolific producer was the firm of Godfrey Phillips during the inter-war period. These were standard sized cards in various colours, with reference letters and numbers on the front, plus a postage stamp. The reverse of the card gave details of an exchange scheme for other stamps or collectors' gifts. Thousands of different varieties have been recorded but the cards are frankly unattractive.

Lambert & Butler **Interesting Sidelights on the Work of the GPO**, 1939 (G, set of 50)

Very different is the set of POSTAGE STAMPS issued by W Duke, Sons & Co in about 1889. These are pictures in superb colour, showing, in the main, scenes relating to the mail. There is a nice touch on the card depicting a country post office as the artist has conveniently included in the foreground a packing case of Duke's cigarettes. Even more appropriate for the cigarette card collector, however, are two other cards. One shows a group of three boys swopping their Duke's stamp cards and the other pictures a well-dressed man, holding a cigarette packet, being accosted by a schoolboy demanding the card inside!

The postage stamps are stuck to the front of the cards in rectangular boxes and the backs come with two types of wording. The first makes the claim that each stamp ranges in value from one cent to one dollar and the second, even more extravagantly, takes the value up to two dollars and fifty cents. The statement goes on to say, 'not only the beginner but the owner of a large collection will find amongst our stamps such as he could never find before.'

Equal in beauty to the Duke cards but, alas, not incorporating real stamps, are the stamp card sets issued on the Continent by Liebig. The series catalogued by Fada as no.630 shows three or more stamps of Bulgaria, Denmark, Greece, Romania, Serbia and Sweden, together with a scene from the country of origin and a

Liebig (F 630) **Postage Stamps**, 1900 (F, set of 6 extra large)

child dressed in national costume. Not quite so well printed but showing a good range of unusual stamps is the series of 100 POSTAGE STAMPS – RAREST VARIETIES, distributed in South Africa by African Tobacco Manufacturers. Not surprisingly, the Cape triangular is one of those included.

African Tobacco **Postage Stamps-Rarest Varieties**, 1929 (J, set of 100 medium)

Delivering the mail

In 1913 the Australian brands of Wills' cigarettes packed an interesting series of ROYAL MAIL cards, which are entirely different to the Ogden's set of the same name. A British issue with an international theme is Salmon & Gluckstein's THE POST IN VARIOUS COUNTRIES*. The 48 cards show methods of letter carrying in many unusual and colourful parts of the world. Although the cards are hard to find and expensive, it is worth trying to include one or two in a philatelic theme collection.

Another rare series is A TOUR ROUND THE WORLD* with postcard back, issued by F & J Smith. Each card purports to be mailed from a different foreign location and the messages cleverly make reference to Smith's tobacco products. Much easier to get hold of is Lambert & Butler's INTERESTING SIDELIGHTS ON THE WORK OF THE GPO and, although the majority of the cards deal with telephonic and telegraphic communication, there are many items to delight the postal enthusiast. The pair of cards numbered 37 and 38 show firstly stamps being printed, and then the reeling of rolls for vending machines. On card 29 the artist delightfully depicts a mail van standing alongside an aircraft

DEAR SIR—

WILL GET THERE QUICKEST!

LAST ROUND.

FRENCH LETTER CARRIER

SIX ANNAS

MEXICAN MAIL.

PONY EXPRESS

POSTE

ZULU MAIL.

IRISH CHANNEL MAIL.

POSTAGE

20 Cent.

POST OFFICE

COUNTRY POST OFFICE.

DUKE'S CIGARETTES

MAIL CAR INTERIOR

POSTE 25 REPUBLIQUE FRANCAISE

NEDERLAND

GIVE US THAT CARD MISTER!

GOT ANY DUKE'S STAMP CARDS.

Duke **Postage Stamps**, c1889 (D, per card)

Delivering the mail and the first human letter

Top to bottom

Right row: Player **British Empire Series**, 1904 (G, set of 50)
Wills **Railway Equipment**, 1939 (C, set of 50)

Middle row: Player **British Empire Series**, 1904 (G, set of 50)
Wills **Do You Know 2nd Series**, 1924 (D, set of 50)
Lambert & Butler **Interesting Sidelights on the Work of the GPO**, 1939 (G, set of 50)

Left row: Wills (BAT) **Riders of the World**, c1926 (G, set of 50)
Churchman **In Town Tonight**, 1938 (C, set of 50)

about to depart for the Shetland Islands.

Although airmail saved an enormous amount of time, it was expensive, and pre-war the steamship provided the basic means for carrying international mail. Many of the ships featured in Wills' two large sets of FAMOUS BRITISH LINERS were used in this way. Overland the railway system provided a fast and economical service and in Churchman's RAILWAY WORKING, card no.22 illustrates the device used for picking up and dropping mail bags. Wills similarly included this apparatus in their RAILWAY EQUIPMENT

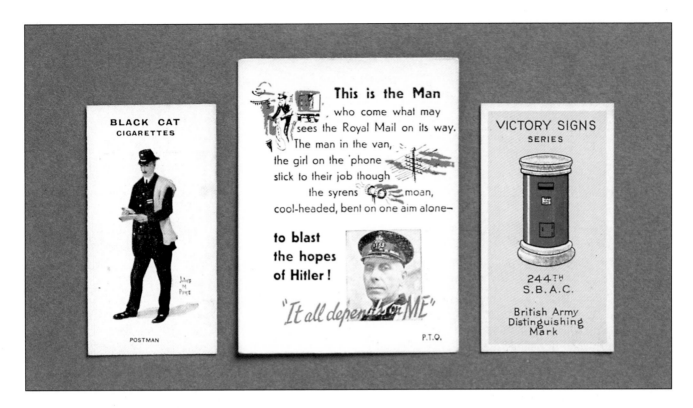

series and also show the inside of a typical mail sorting coach. Pattreiouex's fine photographic series of BRITISH RAILWAYS pictures another Travelling Post Office on card no.13.

Other cards to fit this theme can be found in Player's BRITISH EMPIRE SERIES, including the strange sight of a New South Wales postman on skis! The same firm's set of CYCLING shows the more familiar post office bicycle on card no.11 and in RIDERS OF THE WORLD there is a picture of a Mongolian postman. In more familiar dress and surroundings is the postman in Carreras' TYPES OF LONDON. Ardath's wartime issue of IT ALL DEPENDS ON ME praises the work of post office employees on the card entitled 'On The

Post Office Front'. Of historical significance are the Wills' CALENDAR cards for 1911 and 1912, which give the then current postal rates on the reverse. The same firm's DO YOU KNOW 2ND SERIES illustrates a postcard addressed to W D & H O Wills, Bristol, cancelled with a neat postmark for 1923. Finally, turn to card no.6 in Churchman's set of IN TOWN TONIGHT to find Mr W Reginald Bray, who sent himself through the post and thus became the first human letter.

There are, of course, many more cards that can be traced to fit the philatelic theme. Hopefully, the above examples will have given some idea of the scope and interest that thematic collecting can provide.

Left to right:
Carreras **Types of London**, 1919 (I, set of 80)
Ardath **It All Depends on Me**, c1940 (F, set of 24)
Morris **Victory Signs**, 1928 (E, set of 50)

An insert with postal rates on the reverse.
Wills **Calendar 1912**, 1911 (C, per card)

CHAPTER 10

NOVELTIES AND RELATED EPHEMERA

Over the years there have been many debates in the various journals devoted to collecting cigarette and trade cards, as to what is or is not 'cartophilic'. In other words, what items may properly be included in reference books and catalogues and thus be suitable objects for collectors to acquire. Some of the most distinguished cartophilists have put forward definitions but not one has yet succeeded in laying down parameters which have gained universal approval. Of course, what people want to collect is their own affair and any form of regimentation would be wholly unacceptable. But the compilers of the Cartophilic Society's *World and Trade Indexes* do have a massive problem in deciding what items to classify and what to ignore.

In previous chapters we have taken a very straightforward view of what is a 'card'. Because many thousands of series have been issued with an enormous range of subject matter, there is no reason why a conventional card collector should ever feel bored or frustrated. But even for collectors who like to keep things simple, there can be great fun in exploring the byways and fringe areas of the cartophilic world – and

beyond. After all, cigarette cards were distributed in packets, boxes or tins, so this is one area that collectors might find adds background and extra interest. The cards themselves were a form of advertisement for the issuing firm, thus a look at other promotional items or point of sale material might help to put the cards in their proper context.

In this chapter we shall try to scratch the surface of some of these related areas. Before that, however, there are many unusual items to record that were actually packed with cigarettes and other commodities.

SILKS

Inserts made of material with printed, woven or embroidered designs are usually referred to as 'silks', although frequently the fabric used was not silk. A number of tobacco companies issued these items, sometimes with, but often without, a paper or card backing. The *Gentlewoman Magazine* was among the first to issue silk pictures when they included them with their Christmas editions during the 1890s. Many

Kinney **Novelties*** (die-cut), c1888 (B, per card)

---

page 132

A selection of items that can add interest to a collection of cards, *top to bottom*

Left row:
Duke Cameo cigarette carton, complete with cigarettes (E, per packet)
Wills **Miniatures – Oval Medallions***, 1914 (G, per item)
Wills Woodbine dominoes tin, complete (E, per tin)
Wills Gold Flake playing cards, complete (B, per pack)
Middle row:
Player Hand Made Navy Cut cigarette tin (G, per tin)
United Kingdom Tobacco **Metal Soldiers***, c1935 (D, per item)

Fry Cocoa advertisement postcard (D, per postcard)
Cope **Toy Models** (The Country Fair), c1925 (C, set of 25 large)

Right row:
Kinney **Novelties*** (die cut), c1888 (B, per card)
Record Cigarette Co **The 'Talkie' cigarette card**, c1934 (G, per item)
Cohen Weenen **Celebrities – Gainsborough I***
(in metal frame), c1902 (G, per medium card)
Wills **Happy Families*** (boxed), c1932 (I, set of 32 large)

Themans **Regimental Badges B3**, c1914 (C, per silk)

Collecting silks has a very strong following

Phillips, *left to right:*

Old Masters*
(Set 4), c1913
(A, per medium silk)
County Cricket Badge,
c1921 (D, per medium silk)
Ceramic Art, c1925
(G, set of 47 medium)

others followed their example but the firm most associated with silks is that of Godfrey Phillips. Taking into account different printings and sizes they issued over 100 series between 1910 and 1925.

The most suitable subjects were those that required no printed commentary, so flags, tartans, heraldic devices, army badges, regimental colours, birds and butterflies were among those that appeared. Several sets of OLD MASTERS* were issued, as reproductions of famous paintings showed up extremely well on the silk fabric. Also highly collected are the series of FOOTBALL COLOURS* and COUNTY CRICKET BADGES which Phillips distributed in the early '20s. CERAMIC ART was one of the last series to be produced and included within this set are many wonderful examples of pottery and porcelain.

J Wix & Sons is another tobacco company whose silks are highly prized. They produced some delightful flag and flower series from about 1933. The latter are especially sought after and as the silks were contained in small folders it was possible to print descriptions of the flowers depicted. R J Lea produced some paper backed silks, of which BUTTERFLIES AND MOTHS* issued with Golden Knight cigarettes are

particularly handsome. Muratti, Salmon & Gluckstein, John Sinclair, Robert Sinclair and Themans & Co are among other British tobacco houses that issued silk inserts. Some overseas manufacturers also used this format, with the American Tobacco Company issuing several fine series. BAT issued half a dozen sets in Australia using the Wills name and these are also generally very attractive.

NOVELTY INSERTS

Many and varied were the items that were packed with cigarettes. We have already noted one or two of the companies, such as Wills, who issued sectional series of cards. The West Country firm of Anstie issued six sets in this form between 1935 and 1938. When assembled, they are quite superb and include scenes of STONEHENGE, WELLS CATHEDRAL and WINDSOR CASTLE. Ardath also used the concept a couple of times and their 48 card series of the EMPIRE FLYING-BOAT is a favourite with many collectors. Ogden's and Churchman's SECTIONAL CYCLING MAP and Edwards, Ringer & Bigg's WAR MAP, WESTERN FRONT also form part of this category.

One of the strangest items issued was a mini-gramophone record of about 70mm square. These were issued by the Record Cigarette Co

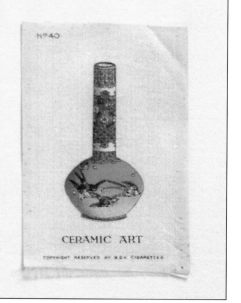

and when played featured sportsmen and other celebrities either talking or performing for their fans. Slightly larger mini-discs were also issued by some trade firms and are equally scarce. Another oddity was the set of toy soldiers, or 'flats' as they are generally called, that were issued by the United Kingdom Tobacco Co with their Greys cigarettes. They are very well made, include mounted and foot soldiers, and are thought to represent troops that fought at the Battle of Balaklava in 1854.

A really beautiful insert was that provided by BAT with Wills' Three Castles cigarettes and supplied in tins for HM Ships between 1912 and 1914. Known as MINIATURES – OVAL MEDALLIONS*, they consist of enamelled portraits of ladies reproduced from famous paintings. A frame could be obtained from the manufacturers by collecting coupons which were also packed with the miniatures. A few years earlier, however, Cohen Weenen had actually issued

small portrait photos in metal frames with their Gainsborough cigarettes. The cards depicted actors, actresses and other celebrities and there was even a pull-out stand at the back so the framed card could be placed on the mantelpiece.

Push-out cards were a novelty item tried by one or two firms but especially by Ogden's. Their BIRDS EGGS, BRITISH BIRDS and CHILDREN OF ALL NATIONS from 1923/24, were pierced round the outline of the design so that they could be pushed out to give a three dimensional effect. Major Drapkin had previously used a similar technique with SOLDIERS AND THEIR UNIFORMS* but the most colourful die-cut cards were those produced by the US firm of Kinney Bros. Many different shapes were used, such as a cigar box, wine glass, watch case, butterfly and even the cob of a sweetcorn.

Of more conventional size and shape were the bronze metal plaques put out by the International Tobacco Co in 1934. Titled FAMOUS

Butterflies are an excellent subject for silk cards.
Lea **Butterflies and Moths***, c1924 (G, set of 12 medium)

Kinney **Novelties*** (die-cut), c1888 (B, per card)

WINDSOR CASTLE

Anstie produced some of the best sectional series of cards

Anstie **Windsor Castle**, 1937 (D, set of 10)

BUILDINGS AND MONUMENTS OF BRITAIN, they were issued in small cellophane envelopes and featured well-known landmarks, such as the Albert Memorial and York Minster. Whitbread also used metal for their first three series of INN SIGNS, although they turned to conventional board for the later series. Circular and oval shaped cards were issued by Phillips, Rothmans and Carreras and both Cope and Mitchell distributed cards that could be made into models. The Cope series consisted of 25 large cards entitled TOY MODELS and depicted a country fair, whereas Mitchell's VILLAGE MODELS SERIES was produced in both standard and large sizes. Naturally, the tobacconist and newsagent shop in the 'village' had a sign outside exhorting patrons to 'Smoke Mitchell's'.

Carreras also put out a scenic model series plus many other inventive items. In the period just before World War I they issued up to 200 small paper booklets in the BLACK CAT LIBRARY series. Then, during the war itself, they produced THE HANDY ENGLISH-FRENCH DICTIONARY with a calendar for 1915 on the last page. Presumably, the phrases were to assist our troops fighting in France. Then after the 1939/45 war they overcame the paper shortage by printing pictures on the inner slides of their Turf cigarette packets. The slides could be saved as issued or the pictures cut out to the regular shape of cigarette cards.

Over the years manufacturers have produced

many thousands of different inserts for information or promotional purposes and these have now become quite collectable. Into this category also fall the many types of gift coupons, that, for a time in the 1930s, actually replaced cards in many brands of cigarettes. Among the earliest are the leaflets and coupons issued by Ogden's in 1901, in connection with their album and gift schemes. Many of the later coupons picture on the front one of the gifts available, with a listing of other items on the reverse. Inserts have often been used to advise smokers of other products, new brands, money saving offers and price changes.

CARD GAMES

Cards of beauties and actresses with playing cards inset were popular around the turn of the century. Because duty was payable on packs of cards, these items could only be used in export brands. Later on, the duty problem was avoided by inserting miniature cards too small to attract duty. This was usually as part of a promotion to exchange sets for full sized packs or other gifts. Wills, Carreras and J Wix used this ploy regularly during the 1930s. Besides miniature

playing cards Ogden's also issued dominoes. Usually, but not always, they had the picture of an actress on the back. Card games were another favourite and Wills and Carreras both issued different versions of Happy Families. One of the earliest card games issued was the set of DOMINOES* put out by Carter's Little Liver Pills around 1910.

It was Carreras, however, who really dominated the 'games' market. Their other issues were ALICE IN WONDERLAND, BATTLE OF WATERLOO, FORTUNE TELLING, THE GREYHOUND RACING GAME and THE 'NOSE' GAME. Churchman's FRISKY and Major Drapkin's THE GAME OF SPORTING SNAP followed a similar format to the Carreras issues but were produced in limited numbers and are now quite scarce.

An interesting sideline is to collect the packs of playing cards that could be obtained in exchange for the miniature cards. The tobacco companies also issued dozens of different style packs of cards for promotional purposes and a type collection of some of these makes a colourful show in an album. One of the modern scarcities in this field is the boxed set of playing cards issued to pensioners and employees by Wills in 1986 to mark their 200th anniversary.

A PARK DRIVE GIFT
195 Coupons

CYCLING GOGGLES
SAFETY GLASS

Many attractive coupons were issued during the coupon war
Gallaher **Park Drive Gift Coupon**, c1930
(A, per coupon)

Carreras inserted many excellent card games with their products
Carreras **Alice In Wonderland**, 1930
(H, set of 48 large)

Collecting errors and varieties is a very interesting sideline

Top to bottom

Left row:
Wills **Radio Celebrities** (1st series), 1934 (B, a pair)

First & second cards, middle row:
Wills **Household Hints**, 1936 (B, a pair)

Third card, middle row:
Carreras **Famous Airmen & Airwomen**, 1936 (A, the card)

Right row:
Player **Footballers 1928**, 1928 (B, a pair)

ERRORS AND VARIETIES

Although the compilers of cigarette and trade cards went to a great deal of trouble to ensure that both pictures and text were accurate, inevitably there were some mistakes made. A few of these error cards can add interest to a collection and it is always worth checking your own collection just in case you can spot a mistake. Possibly the most famous error concerns card no.43 in Player's series of DANDIES. This depicted Benjamin Disraeli in

the series **IN THE PUBLIC EYE**. The first card issued spelt his name wrong on the front and listed only three of his four cricketers' doubles. This latter mistake was subsequently corrected but the mis-spelt name remained.

Sometimes variations were due to an untimely death, as was the case with comedian John Tilley, who appeared in Wills' second series of **RADIO CELEBRITIES**. He died shortly after the cards were issued and a revised printing was made to reflect this fact. The transfer of footballers from one club to another was a perennial problem for compilers and a typical example is J McStay, featured in Mitchell's **SCOTTISH FOOTBALLERS**. His club was shown on both front and back captions as Celtic but when he moved on to Hamilton Academicals only the caption on the back of the card was altered.

Mistakes during the printing process also turn up from time to time. Sometimes a colour is omitted from a print run and on other occasions the backs might not be correctly aligned with the fronts. There have been some extraordinary cases where the back of the card is from a completely different series to the front. Printers' trials and proofs find their way onto the market from time to time and it is nice to mount these in an album next to the issued card. Mr W Bryce Neilson has written three booklets on errors and varieties and they are essential reading for anyone interested in this aspect of the hobby.

ALBUMS

Quite a few tobacco manufacturers issued special albums or folders to go with their card series and these could usually be purchased from tobacconists for a penny or two. Some, such as the 'sticky back' albums from Player and Wills, were fairly modest affairs, but others were well-made hardback items. The concept has been continued by Imperial Tobacco with their cigar cards issued since 1975 and also by many trade firms such as Barratt and Brooke Bond. It is one of the quirks of collecting that once the cards are glued into their special album, both items become virtually unsaleable. Anyone who decides to buy such items, however, would be able to put together an interesting collection very cheaply.

1826, standing on Westminster Bridge, with the Houses of Parliament and Big Ben behind him. Unfortunately, the artist had overlooked the fact that Big Ben had not been built at that date so a second printing was made with the clock tower erased. This, however, left a smudge in the background and eventually the card had to be completely redrawn.

A similar situation arose with Wills' **HOUSEHOLD HINTS** produced in 1936. The original caption referred to 'Cleaning A Thermos Flask', but 'Thermos' was a proprietary brand and the manufacturers objected. A second card was issued but only the caption on the back was altered so eventually a third printing had to be made. Another classic is **FIGURES OF FICTION** from Carreras where Uncle Tom was at first pictured with a black face and black hands but white feet!

The artist responsible for Player's **FOOTBALLERS** 1928, whilst correcting an error on card no.24, somehow managed to make another. B O Male, the Welsh international, was originally pictured with white shorts and whilst these were successfully changed to black, his red socks were at the same time mysteriously bleached to white. So whichever of the two varieties you have there is an error on it. Another sportsman to suffer a similar fate was cricketer Maurice Nichols, featured by Phillips in

Albums are usually more valuable when the cards have not been stuck in

Left to right:

Radio Review album for **Broadcasting Stars*** (Set of 36) with cards stuck in, 1935 (E, per item)
Wills album for **Radio Celebrities** (1st Series) with cards stuck in, 1938 (B, per item)
Player album for **Cricketers 1938** unused, 1938 (D, per item)

Liebig (F 1045) **Military Manoeuvres in Italy**, 1912, inserted in special corner slot album, cover shown on left (C, set of 6 extra large)

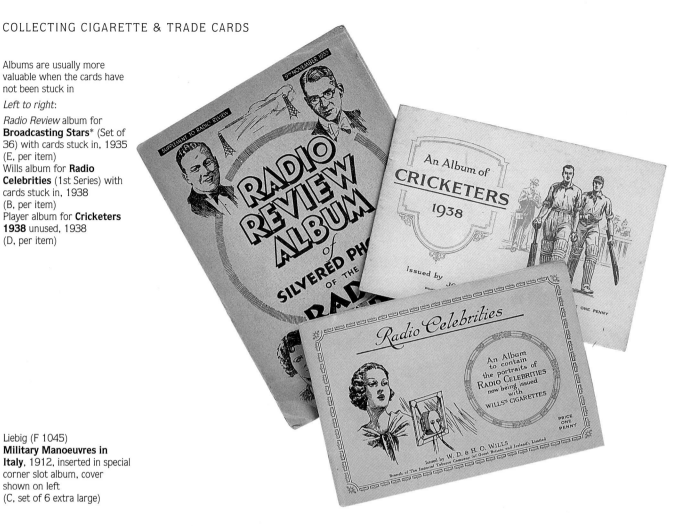

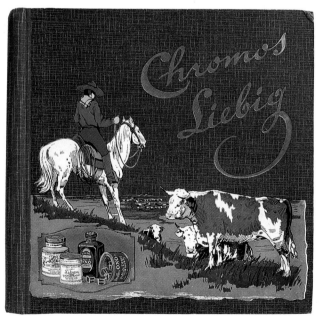

The albums issued by German manufacturers were often lavish and sometimes an integral part of the card series. South African and Dutch manufacturers also issued some first rate albums in which their cards could be housed. The album for OUR SOUTH AFRICAN NATIONAL PARKS issued by United Tobacco Companies, for example, is really a book and the cards when stuck in form the illustrations. Sometimes extra text or illustrations are given as was the case with Sarony's album for AROUND THE MEDITERRANEAN. This provided a handy map plotting the route followed by the cards.

Empty special albums have in recent years become quite collectable and prices reflect the fact that there are not that many of them about in clean, unused condition. Corner slot types are not favoured but those issued by Wills and John Player for adhesive cards and some of the early Brooke Bond items are worth looking out for.

ADVERTISING POSTCARDS

Some tobacco firms did actually include cards with postcard backs in their larger cartons of cigarettes. Godfrey Phillips' FILM STARS* and Sarony's CINEMA STARS are possibly the best known of these. R J Lea prepared 24 postcard versions from their OLD ENGLISH POTTERY AND PORCELAIN series but these were not packed with cigarettes and were sold through tobacconists' shops. Postcards published by Raphael Tuck and other leading manufacturers, which actually depict tobacco products, are highly sought after.

Many trade firms issued picture postcards and although some were given away with periodicals or made available to customers through grocery outlets, the majority were sold to the public in the same way as ordinary postcards. Even these items are, however, listed in the Cartophilic Society's *British Trade Index*, thus providing a point of reference for collectors to the thousands of cards that are available.

The most desirable items tend to be the postcards that illustrate reproduction posters, especially if a prominent artist prepared the design. J S Fry with their chocolate products, Hudson's Soap and Colman's Mustard are among those that are keenly sought after. Many similar

style cards were produced on the Continent and in the USA with Suchard, Cacao Bensdorp and the Singer Sewing Machine Co among the more prominent.

Some of the tea firms, such as Lipton and CWS, issued scenes of overseas tea plantations, whilst Horniman's cards are of British views. Cadbury, with the model village of Bournville, and Lever Brothers with scenes of Port Sunlight, produced cards that had the dual purpose of advertising a product and establishing the social credentials of the issuers. Other cards usually found listed in dealers' catalogues are the charming fruit studies issued by Chivers & Sons and postcard reproductions of those evocative Guinness posters that appeared either side of the Second World War.

Reward cards are closely associated with postcards and were often issued by manufacturers such as Cadbury and Nectar Tea. Probably the largest issuers, however, were the various educational authorities and these cards can usually be purchased for a pound or two. Although not strictly qualifying as advertising postcards, mention must be made of those cards featuring an urchin begging for a cigarette card. These are guaranteed to bring back special memories for the more mature collectors!

Many cartophilists also collect advertising postcards

Left to right: Singer **Advertising Postcard***, c1905 (C, the card) Guinness **Famous Guinness for Strength Posters***, 1951 (F, set of 6 extra large)

page 143
A selection of cigarette
packets and tins, c1900 to
1950

Many excellently produced
commercial cards are available
today
Golden Era **Classic MG
Series**, 1992
(B, set of 7 large)

One of the most famous sets
never to be issued
Wills **Waterloo**, unissued
(I, per card)

COMMERCIAL CARDS

When cards were issued in great profusion at no cost to the recipient there was little reason for the commercial sale of picture cards. At least, not in the style of cigarette and trade cards. Following the conclusion of the Second World War materials were in short supply and money was tight so, again, there was little market for commercially produced cards. The confectionery and tea companies partially made up for the loss of cigarette cards in the 1950s and '60s but as these were often directed at the juvenile market, many adults gradually drifted away from the hobby.

It was the chewing gum manufacturers who first sensed that there was a market for selling cards. The gum gradually disappeared from the packets and led the way to commercial printers selling packets of cards and stickers which children (and, let it be said, some adults) could fix into albums. In recent years it has grown to become a huge market with the traditional subjects of football, film and TV-related series being augmented by cards on golf, cricket, snooker and classic cars. In the United States, where there has been a phenomenal growth in card collecting, the market is dominated by the baseball enthusiast.

The scarcity of rare, old cigarette cards and the growing demand for framed sets of cards, have been the main reasons for the issue of reproduction cards. As prices of scarce material escalated so the risk of forgeries became more significant. The advantage of reproduction cards is that they are clearly marked as such on the reverse, so there is little risk of anyone buying them in mistake for the real thing. They have also creamed off some of the demand from the framing market, which was starting to take a large number of original cards out of circulation.

Some experienced collectors have mixed feelings about the way the card market is developing. But it has to be said that many of the cards that are being sold commercially are of a high standard and there is no question that they are fulfilling a real need. In the 1930s,

when over 100 different sets were being issued each year, the collecting of cards was at its peak. Today we are seeing similar enthusiasm, notwithstanding the wide variety of leisure interests that are currently available. At present, the range of subject matter is still fairly narrow but this may improve with time.

Series of cards that were produced by the tobacco companies but never inserted in packets, are of interest to most collectors. Some were released in large numbers and are not too difficult to obtain but others, such as Wills' WATERLOO and LIFE OF KING EDWARD VIII, are extremely rare.

PACKETS AND TINS

Packaging and containers are items most people take very much for granted. Tins have long been of interest to collectors, but it is only recently that there has been an appreciation of other forms of packaging. Cigarette packets are no exception. At first they were flimsy paper affairs and even when the hull and slide type was invented, there was no real thought in most people's minds of keeping them as a collectable item.

There is a close association between the cigarette card and the packet and not only because it was the medium through which the card was issued. Before descriptive texts became common, cards were often used to promote the brands of cigarettes or one of the other products sold by the manufacturer. Through to the end of the Edwardian period there were some wonderful brand names such as Society Girl from Morris, May Blossom, Royal Salute and Trumpeter from Lambert & Butler, Nutcracker from Gallaher, Sweet Lips from Cadle, Taddy's famous Myrtle Grove, Cope's Rosebud and Smith's Wild Geranium, Morning Gallop and Rustic Beauty.

Because of the short life of many brands and also the high destruction factor, these early packs are rare and expensive. Many of the brands that enjoyed a long life can, however, be acquired without great difficulty. In this category are Wills' Gold Flake and Wild Woodbine, the famous Player's Navy Cut with the sailor's head trademark, Churchman's

MURATTI'S "YOUNG LADIES" CIGARETTES

SNAKE CHARMER CIGARETTES

HIGH CLASS

SPECIAL BLEND

SALMON & GLUCKSTEIN, Ld. LONDON

HIGNETT'S Golden Butterfly

12 CIGARETTES FINEST QUALITY

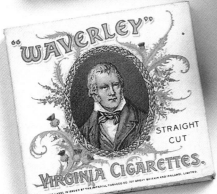

"WAVERLEY" STRAIGHT CUT VIRGINIA CIGARETTES.

THIS LABEL IS ISSUED BY THE IMPERIAL TOBACCO CO. (OF GREAT BRITAIN AND IRELAND), LIMITED.

MEADOWLAND CIGARETTES

A SUPERIOR BLEND OF THE FINEST VIRGINIA TOBACCOS

OGDEN'S "ROBIN" CIGARETTES

FAMILIES HALF-ROUGE WATERLOO WATERLOO TAVISTOCK

BLENDUM OROSHADE DESTINGER WELLINGS BALAKLAVA

THE "GREYS" SIZE TWO

SILK CUT VIRGINIA

MAJOR DRAPKIN & C° LONDON
BRANCH OF THE UNITED KINGDOM TOBACCO C° Lᵀᴰ

OUR BELIEF, THE FINEST LEAF

Kensitas CIGARETTES Extra Size

OGDEN'S GUINEA GOLD CIGARETTES

Beware of Imitations

British made by British Labour

"GOLD FLAKE" CIGARETTES

W.D. & H.O. WILLS' GOLD FLAKE HONEY DEW

W.D. & H.O. WILLS

BRISTOL & LONDON

WILD WOODBINE CIGARETTES

W.D. & H.O. WILLS

BRISTOL & LONDON

CORK TIPPED TRADE MARK

CRAVEN "A"

VIRGINIA CIGARETTES

LARWOOD,
NOTTS AND TEST TEAM.

Phillips **Package Designs***
(orange frame line), c1932
(B, per item)

Right:

Showcard for Byron
Cigarettes, produced by
Walker's Tobacco Pty Ltd,
c1950 (E, per item),
(size 370 x 240mm)

Tenner, Park Drive from Gallaher, Black Cat from Carreras, and Ogden's Guinea Gold, Tabs and Robin. In the trade field sweet cigarette and candy stick packets also have quite a following these days but, as with cigarettes, the early ones are quite elusive.

Packages with cards printed on them have been issued by a number of trade firms. Phillips also tried out this technique during the coupon era and repeated the experiment between 1948 and 1954 with their Sports package designs. Due to the lower standard of board used and the absence of descriptive text, these items are not very popular.

Tins, being more durable, had more chance of survival but, of course, there were far fewer of them. Tobacco tins are available in greater number but for cigarettes Three Castles and Navy Cut can usually be found fairly easily. Similarly Black Cat, Kensitas, De Reszke and The Greys are brands that are fairly common. But if you can track down a Salmon & Gluckstein Snake Charmer tin, Churchman's Tortoiseshell or Muratti's After Lunch, then you will have an item to enjoy and treasure.

ADVERTISING MATERIAL

Dummy packets, booklets, leaflets, show cards, posters, and magazine advertisements are all attractive items to collect. The latter items can be framed and hung on the wall and provide variety to framed cigarette cards. Some interesting booklets have been published from time to time by the tobacco and trade companies. Among the most desirable are the *Smoke-Room Booklets* of which fourteen were published by Cope Bros in the 1890s. Letterheads and bill heads of the tobacco companies are other items that can sometimes be found at ephemera fairs. Whist and Bridge scorecards, menu cards, cricket and football fixture cards are among the practical items that

have been used for promotional purposes.

Beer mats, drip mats, metal trays, ash trays and a host of games have been manufactured for the public house trade or for use as promotional items. Shove-halfpenny boards, crib boards, tins of dominoes, dice, football and cricket games can all add novelty and interest to a card collection. For those who wish to delve deeper into smoking collectables there are cigarette papers, holders, cases, boxes and dispensers, cigar bands and labels, pipes, lighters, vesta cases, matchboxes, book matches, snuff boxes and a lot more besides.

Whatever you decide to collect from this huge kaleidoscope of material, the small picture-card which records, informs and delights, can look forward to a continuing future as the basis of a vibrant and worthwhile hobby.

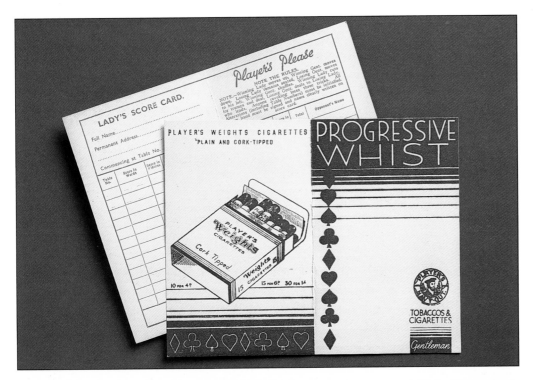

The tobacco companies produced many different promotional items

Player **Whist Score** Cards*, c1940 (C, the pair)

Display sign for Smith's Studio Cigarettes, c1910
(G, per item),
(Size 260 x 350mm)

CARD CONDITION GRADING GUIDE

The card grading guide as recommended by the Cartophilic Society of Great Britain is, with their permission, set out below.

1 Excellent
Cards have been handled but only to a minimum extent and with extreme care, allowing no blemishes whatsoever.

2 Very Good
Completely clean cards back and front, with no damage. In particular corners would be untouched, but edges might show slight signs of wear.

3 Good
Minor blemishes might be visible, ie due to age, and there could be slight damage to corners.

4 Fair
A card from one of the above categories, but with one defect, such as a crack, dirty mark, damaged back.

5 Poor
A card with more than one defect (as in 'Fair'), or with one very serious defect, such as back completely missing.

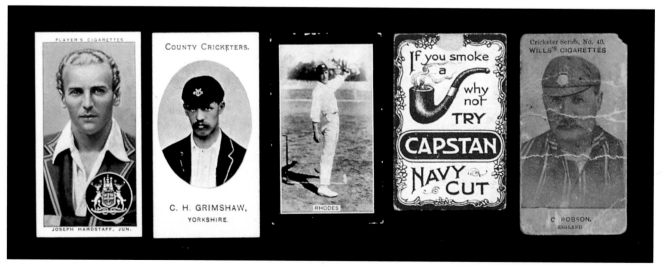

1   2   3   4   5

GLOSSARY

The source for most of the terms defined below has been *Cartophilic Reference Book No.8* published by the Cartophilic Society in 1948. The co-operation of the Cartophilic Society in making available the use of their reference book is much appreciated.

Actresses The description generally applied to untitled series of cards where captions denote the names of the female personalities depicted.

Adhesive backs Cards treated with a dried glutinous substance to permit fixing after damping to an album page. Generally referred to as 'sticky backs'.

Adopted title A title bestowed on a series of cards lacking a printed title. Where a series carries a printed name it is referred to as 'titled'.

Advertisement backs Back of card carrying advertising and not text descriptive of picture.

Advertisement cards Picture cards, usually miniature reproductions of other advertising matter, as distinct from a sequence of cards devoted to one subject.

Albums clause A printed statement, usually on card backs, stating that an album has been published in which cards may be stored.

Alike series Cards showing identical subjects, and issued by several manufacturers, bearing their respective names or trademarks.

Anonymous Of unknown, or anavowed authorship. No maker's name appearing anywhere. This situation occurs with certain plain back material, but is also met deliberately prepared, where makers are using more than one trading name.

ATC Clause Cards bearing the imprint or name of the American Tobacco Company.

Backlisted A series in which a list of the different subjects appears on the card's back.

BAT An abbreviation for British-American Tobacco Company Limited, founded in 1902 by the American Tobacco Company and The Imperial Tobacco Company (of Great Britain and Ireland) Limited.

Beauties The description generally applied to untitled series of cards where the female personalities depicted are unnamed. This designation still applies even if the identities of the persons depicted have been traced.

Brand issue Denotes a series on which a brand or brands are quoted without other indication of the issuer. Cases where the brand is the same as the name of the sponsoring firm are not considered brand issues.

Cartophily The science and practice of collecting cigarette and other trade cards.

Chromo An abbreviation of chromolithography, implying a card or series is printed in several colours by lithography.

Code letters The system devised to distinguish between similar series of cards issued by several different manufacturers. Usually based on a combination of the initial letters of some of the firms using the series.

Collotype A printing process of 'near photographic' type. Making use of the original photographic negative as a master, instead of preparing printing plates or blocks.

Commercial cards Cards or stickers produced specifically for sale as a commercial venture and not having been previously circulated with a product.

Condition In cartophily the manner in which a card has been preserved. The Cartophilic Society have prepared a recommended grading guide for describing the condition of cards which appears as an appendix in this book on page 146.

Coupon A card or slip of paper, packed with cigarettes and having exchangeable value for some commodity.

Descriptive back Card backs carrying text and explaining the picture on the reverse side, or elaborating on the same subject. Text related to goods is called 'advertisement back'.

Error A departure from that which is right and correct. Mainly cartophily is concerned with typographical errors – and their correction, errors in design, whether corrected or not, and errors and omissions of colour, usually proven by a replacement card.

Frame lines The lines drawn round a study or subject, usually rectangular, to provide a border or margin.

Inset Something additional, it may be a line of type, a miniature playing card (playing card inset), or a portrait (portrait inset).

ITC Clause The phrases used by The Imperial Tobacco Company on cards sponsored by their branches, ie, 'Branch of The Imperial Tobacco Co. (of Great Britain and Ireland) Ltd' or 'Issued by The Imperial Tobacco Co. (of Great Britain and Ireland) Ltd', in both cases followed by the branch name – Player, Churchman etc. These phrases signified that the cards had domestic circulation, ie within the British Customs area.

Monochrome Cards printed in one colour or line only. Cards printed in black only are usually described as black and white, whereas monochrome implies some colour other than black has been used.

Multi-backed A series which has different backs or back advertisements, in which subjects can be collected with more than one back, but in which all subjects cannot be collected with all backs.

Narrow card A card narrower than normal, and usually compared with a normal card dealing with the same subject. The term is frequently used to describe normal sized cards which have been cut mechanically to reduce the width, and so make them suitable for insertion in two different sized packings.

Net design A network design background, printed on some card backs and mainly issued by the American Tobacco Company during the Tobacco War period.

Overseas issue A card circulated outside the boundaries of the British Customs and Excise. The point of sale and circulation of the card decides, and not the place of manufacture. In the case of cards bearing the names of the members of the ITC group, this can be confusing as both brand names and trading names are used abroad by BAT. Usually, but not exclusively, cards so issued do not bear the ITC Clause. Cards issued in Eire are a case in point–they sometimes carry the ITC Clause.

Plain back A card without any printing or similar marking on the reverse side to the picture, and circulated in that form.

Playing card inset Cards having a playing card printed in the corner or worked into the design, in miniature. Usually 52 or 53 form a set and in that form only issued overseas.

Pretty girls The description generally applied to untitled series of cards where the captions specify only the first name of the female personality depicted.

Redrawn A subject drawn again through error or unsuitability of the original, generally constituting a variety.

Remainders Cards which are left behind in a cigarette manufacturer's or printer's possession, when issue is stopped. Remainders find their way into dealer's hands, and are accepted by collectors as normal cards or sets.

Reprint A second edition, but usually immediately following the first, ie, without interval, and therefore differing from a re-issue.

Reproduction In cartophily, the term has two broad meanings. A likeness of an original subject, eg a painting or drawing, or a copy of a card or set of cards.

Series An assemblage of cards, prepared as a complete group, which may be arranged either by numbers, identifying title, or other connecting means. The word is commonly used on card backs and signifies the complete issue was made simultaneously.

Silks Inserts and insets printed or woven on silk or other material. May be backed with paper for support, or circulated folded or flat in natural form.

Size Extent of surface. In cartophilic terms size is seldom absolute. It can fluctuate fractionally through mechanics and reference to card dimensions is to the intended sizes. Small (or standard) size – as used by branches of the ITC and many other cigarette manufacturers – is 67mm x 36mm. Large size is 79mm x 67mm and extra large 98mm x 67mm. Cards produced before 1920 have greater latitude in surface, but correspond to the above.

Sticky backs A colloquialism used to describe cards with adhesive backs.

Stiffeners A trade name used to describe enpackaged cards, the implication being that the card stiffens the package, and helps to support a fragile commodity.

Trade cards Most collectors differentiate between cards issued by tobacco companies and those issued with other commodities, although the term is really a misnomer. All cards advertising goods or services may be called trade cards.

Type card A card out of a series and representative of, or characteristic of the whole. Collections of type cards are particularly suitable for early and expensive material and can be instead of, or in addition to, acquiring complete sets.

Unicoloured One colour printing only, for instance, black.

Unissued Cards prepared for issue, but not circulated in a recognised manner. Although specimens or sets may come into the possession of a collector this does not constitute circulation.

Unnumbered A series of cards not possessing numerical sequence, usually found in very old issues.

Vari-backed A series which has different backs or back advertisements, but in which no subject can be collected with more than one back.

Varieties A number of cards nearly-allied to each other, but differing in minor points. The same front with changes in the back matter would constitute a variety, or possibly an error.

Vignettes Usually a print or impression where the shading generally disappears – the fading off outwards being intentional and repeatedly occurring.

Withdrawn A set or part of any set of cards withdrawn from circulation, either for replacement, or for unspecified reasons. A card may be withdrawn through an error occurring in preparation, or because it gives offence.

Woodburytype An obsolete form of printing, by means of warm gelatine, to imitate photography. Rare, and at present only known in classic issues, such as those from Ogden's, Drapkin & Millhoff and Allen & Ginter. Cards appear like real photos, but detection is possible by ridges which show against the light.

BIBLIOGRAPHY

Bagnall, Dorothy, *Collecting Cigarette Cards and Other Trade Issues*, London Cigarette Card Co Ltd, Somerset, 1973

Bason, Frederick T, *Cigarette Card Collectors' Handbook & Guide*, Robert Anscombe & Co Ltd, London, 1938

Cruse, A J, *Cigarette Card Cavalcade*, Vawser & Wiles (London) Ltd, London, 1948

Doggett, Frank, *Cigarette Cards and Novelties*, Michael Joseph, London, 1981

Evans, I O, *Cigarette Cards and How to Collect Them*, Herbert Jenkins, London, 1937

Genders, Roy, *A Guide to Collecting Trade and Cigarette Cards*, Pelham Books, London, 1975

Gurd, Eric, *Prologue to Cigarette Cards*, A W Duncan & Co Ltd, Liverpool, 1942

Mullen, Chris, *Cigarette Pack Art*, Ventura Publishing Ltd, London, 1979

Murray, Martin, *The Story of Cigarette Cards*, Murray Cards (International) Ltd, London, 1987

Reference Books

a Published by the Cartophilic Society of Great Britain:
The Australian & New Zealand Index, Parts 1 & 11
British Trade Index, Parts 1, 11 & 111
The World Index, Parts 1, 11, 111, IV & V

b Published by London Cigarette Card Co Ltd:
Guidebook No.1, Typhoo Tea Cards
Guidebook No.2, F & J Smith Cigarette Cards
Guidebook No.3, American & British Chewing Gum Ltd Cards
Handbook Part I, British Cigarette Card Issues 1888–1919
Handbook Part II, British Cigarette Card Issues 1920–1940
Errors & Varieties, British Trade Cards, W Bryce Neilson

c Published by Murray Cards (International) Ltd:
British Silk Issues (Second Edition), Dorothy Sawyer
Errors & Varieties, British Cigarette Cards Parts 1 & 2, W Bryce Neilson

d Other publishers:
Brooke Bond Picture Cards 'The First Forty Years', A L Waterhouse, published by the author, 1994
The Standard Guide on all Collected Cards (The American Card Catalog), J R Burdick, USA, 1960

Specialist Magazines

Card Times, Magpie Publications, 70 Winifred Lane, Aughton, Ormskirk, Lancs L39 5DL

Cartophilic Notes & News, The Cartophilic Society of Great Britain, Membership Secretary: K F Fox, 116 Hill View Road, Ensbury Park, Bournemouth, BH10 5BJ

Cigarette Card News and Trade Card Chronicle, The London Cigarette Card Co Ltd, Sutton Road, Somerton, Somerset TA11 6QP

Priced Catalogues

Albert's, 113 London Road, Twickenham, TW1 1EE

The London Cigarette Card Co Ltd, Sutton Road, Somerton, Somerset TA11 6QP

Murray Cards (International) Ltd, 51 Watford Way, Hendon Central, London NW4 3JH

INDEX

Page numbers in bold type refer to illustrations